Celebrating Your Scars

LIVING BOLDLY FOR CHRIST!

Theresa Whitfield

with Victoria Sandbrook

All Biblical quotations are from the New International Version,
unless otherwise noted.

Written by Theresa Whitfield with Victoria Sandbrook
Published by Welstar Publications, Inc.
Horace Batson, Publisher
628 Lexington Avenue, Brooklyn, NY 11221.
Phone: (718) 453-6557
Fax: (718) 338-1454
E-mail: publisher@WelstarPublications.com
or editor@WelstarPublications.com
Website: http://www.WelstarPublications.com
ISBN: 978-0-938503-84-2
10 9 8 7 6 5 4 3 2 1
Managing Editor, Kate E. Stephenson
Copy Editor, Joshua Garstka
Book Design/Typography, Kate E. Stephenson
Text set in Palatino Linotype.
Cover Design, John White

*Please note: Some names in this text have been changed to protect the
identities of the innocent and to respect the privacy of all.*

ACKNOWLEDGEMENTS

Giving honor to God, who is the head of my life, the author and finisher of my faith. For without Him I am nothing. My life will forever give God glory.

This book is dedicated to my husband, friend and pastor, Jonathan Whitfield, who is truly my inspiration, my joy, my everything.

I want to thank him for believing in me, not just that I could make it through the attack, but for always believing in me, that I could make it through all of the obstacles seen and unseen. You encouraged me to write, to sing, to soar and to be everything God has created me to be.

I want to thank my children, for always being there, always listening and being my sounding board, when at times I felt I was going half-crazy. For staying grounded and being strong examples of Christ. For not showing a spirit of fear, even though sometimes things were scary. For never giving up. I want to encourage each of you to continue the press, to press toward the mark of the high calling for each of your lives.

I want to thank my mother and my sisters and brothers. For there were times we did not see eye to eye, nor could we understand why we would say or do the things we did. But one thing we do know is that we truly love and care for each other. And that comes from a mother who instilled in us a true sense of family, that we are all we have and we stick together no matter what comes. We are our brothers' and sisters' keepers. Thank you for being a real family and keeping me real.

I want to thank Welstar Publications for wading through the weeds and finding a beautiful story in me to share with the world. Kate, thank you for letting me share, vent, cry, and for praying with me that we can do it. Dr. Batson, you are truly a man of God; for only a man of God can have as much patience as I have seen you display over this year. To Victoria Sandbrook, thank you for helping me find my voice so my words will not only be heard, but also felt. Truly life can be a journey, but what is a journey if you can't tell it, and what is a journey if it can't be heard?

A special thanks to Dr. Bikoff, who I call the number-one plastic surgeon who ever lived. Thank you for believing and acknowledging the God in me. I truly believe God ordained us to meet on that day, July 22, 2007. Thank you for letting Him use you in your gift of healing. Continue to acknowledge Him in all your ways, and He will direct your path.

FOREWORD
by Jennifer McGugins Hill, M.D.

The story you are about to read is a story of triumph. The twenty-second day in the month of July 2007 marked a day of tragedy for Lady Whitfield. You will come to learn that her scars began to form long before her attack. Her story will reflect victory, but it is her understanding of God's grace that has gotten her there.

The attack of Lady Whitfield on July 22, 2007, at Trinity Baptist Church had an effect on all who were involved, including myself. When the screams of horror began, I raced downstairs toward the sounds meeting Yolanda Cooper, the attacker at the door. I recall my sister, who was sitting next to me, saying, "One minute I saw you and the next minute you were gone." The surreal image of Ms. Cooper holding a bloody box cutter was quickly replaced by Lady Whitfield screaming and running toward me, now dressed in a blood-stained white dress. The moments to follow have been outlined in this book and will stay with me forever. Our "meeting at the sink," as I have come to call it, was in the midst of utter chaos. Yet there was a sense of calm and silence within me. I realize that this was the presence of God. This presence has enabled me to remain calm despite the inherent dangers in the multitude of emergencies that I have been called to within my profession. It is this calm and silence that is the whisper of God. This whisper of God, His clarity, His calm and His strength, is our faith. This same strength was given to Lady Whitfield on this day and throughout her journey. It is through His grace that she has gained the victory over this devastating event.

Her story leads its readers through challenge and faith. Where there is fear there is no faith. Lady Whitfield has had every reason to be fearful every day since her attack. Fear comes from being displaced from our comfort zone.

Our comfort zone is dictated by what we know, and this usually is molded by our experiences. Whether it is wealth, beauty, vanity, abuse, neglect, greed, lust, drugs, prostitution, infidelity, it is NOT of God. We are created by God as His children, and He will challenge our comfort zone in an effort to make us who He wants us to be... Better! It is only when we accept the challenges of God and walk by faith will we rid ourselves of fear—will we always be able to do His work. It is a choice that we make. It was no coincidènce that I was sitting toward the rear of the church close enough to hear those screams that day. Our choice of faith over fear and His plans to use us often work together harmoniously. It happened to me on July 22, 2007, at Trinity Baptist Church.

The journey you are about to embark upon reflects the decision to choose His way. This book encourages YOU to embrace the beauty of your scars. God has allowed them to happen for a reason, a purpose.

So I say to you, celebrate them!

CONTENTS

INTRODUCTION: WHO CARES?

I have not come to preach, but hopefully to encourage and inspire those who are trying to find their way through this thing called human life. The importance of this message is not what it achieves as being a good message, but what it sets in motion, "a message with a purpose."

My title chosen for this time must be judged not only by the manner in which it is expressed, but to whom it is addressed and not just addressed to a particular person but to your experiences. I am not sure who I have been preparing this word for. But tap your neighbor and tell them I need this word to shift me to my destiny. (from the sermon "A Need for a Shift")

When I first told a special young woman about my intentions to write this book, I received the shock of my life—her response was simply, "Who cares?" She said to me that in this life we see so many horrible things, nothing is new anymore, so who would really care about my story?

It was like I'd been hit by a ton of bricks.

Who cares?

Those two words communicated a world of hurt and need—that need is why I wanted this message in the world. Who cares? I do. But then I suppose many folks would ask, "Well, who are you?" It's a fair question, when the truth is that so many of us really don't know who we are. To tell the truth, neither did I, until a blessing literally cut me open and revealed my true purpose and destiny to me. So for all of those reading now and wondering, *Well, just who does she think she is?* I can tell you—I am a beautiful child of God, a fearfully and wondrously made woman of purpose, a testimony ready and willing to bear witness to the goodness of

God and to His powerful presence in my life and in the world. But that's not the answer that's important, that's not even the question that needs to be answered.

I want to go back and speak to that two-word question: Who cares?

To God be the glory for He so truly cares about us! *He cares.* Not because of anything we've done, but because we are His children, no matter how we walk away, ignore Him or curse His name. God cares.

But, I think, that special young woman should know that already. As a devoted member of our church, I know her faith in the Lord, and so I know she knows God cares. So still there is something missing. And the missing are all around us.

Today we don't have time to think about how f.i.n.e. we are. And no, those periods aren't typos. The truth of the matter is that most of us are not fine, as in all right, feeling good, peachy keen. No. We aren't. We're all running around f.i.n.e. — freaked out, insecure, neurotic, and emotional. We put up the front like we can handle it (whatever "it" is) when the truth is we are failing and faltering and fading into a pale excuse of an existence. Life is that thing that skitters across us as we are just lying down taking whatever comes. In the 21st century with tsunamis, earthquakes, hurricanes, mudslides, tornadoes and disease raging across the world, we can't seem to catch our breaths. We are living in a constant state of hyperventilation such that we can't even see that we aren't getting any oxygen. We are freaked out by all of the craziness happening around us. We are insecure about our places in the world. We are operating in a constant state of neurosis, stifled by anxiety, obsessed with scandal and gore, compulsive in our excesses and mysteriously tormented in body. We are so emotional that we can no longer process all of the chaos of our minds.

To care, to be concerned, or to look out for our fellow

brothers and sisters seems a luxury that we just can't afford, when it's so hard for us to simply care for ourselves.

I learned this firsthand, as both a victim and a victimizer. Now you might wrinkle your brow at that statement, scratch your chin or tap your forehead thinking, *What does she mean by that? Sister Whitfield a victimizer?* No, I don't mean that I've gone out and assaulted anyone; but I am guilty just as many of us are of neglecting the Golden Rule, the highest of all the Commandments—Love the Lord your God with all of your heart, and love your neighbor as you love yourself. When we ignore this greatest assignment from God, we become both victimizers and our own victims. And it is so easy to do. To love your neighbor as yourself requires that you love yourself. To love your God with your whole heart requires that you are in touch with your heart and that it is open to not only give but to receive love.

Who cares?

If you don't care about yourself, you can't care about anyone else. And if you can't care about anyone else then you can't love God, because God is love and demands love and requires that we love one another.

Who cares?

My brothers and sisters, I come to you to say that you must care. If you don't care, really and truly, who will? We are all thirsty for each other, and we do not know how to quench that thirst, because we have lost sight of the most important part of our humanity—caring for each other. Humans are social creatures that cannot survive without each other. And when we hurt each other, we harm only ourselves. We are caught in a cycle of destruction that we ourselves cannot escape from without some divine intervention.

God cares. But unless we do, unless we can stare f.i.n.e. in the face and say *I want my life back and I want it more abundantly in the name of Jesus Christ!*, unless we can see each other and care for each other, God cannot help us.

Then there is f.e.a.r. Again, those periods are not typos. Fear is nothing more than false evidence appearing real, and I know this because in 2 Timothy 1:7-10, the Bible declares:

> *For God has not given us a spirit of fear, but of power and of love and of a sound mind.*
>
> *Therefore do not be ashamed of the testimony of our Lord, nor of me His prisoner, but share with me in the sufferings for the gospel according to the power of God, who has saved us and called us with a holy calling, not according to our works, but according to His own purpose and grace which was given to us in Christ Jesus before time began, but has now been revealed by the appearing of our Savior Jesus Christ, who has abolished death and brought life and immortality to light through the gospel.*

God has given us life such that we may live it more abundantly with a sober boldness to declare His good works and proclaim His name forever, always and everywhere. When I say sober here, I don't mean before we've hit the bottle—no. I'm talking about a clear, sane mind. We are not meant to be tormented by fear, debilitated by doubt, or accosted by our own shortcomings. Life is a gift and it gives us the opportunity, and responsibility, to give something back by becoming more. More than just existing to say you lived. How about saying you lived with purpose, in purpose, and full of purpose?

You know, beliefs have the power to create and they have the power to destroy. For too long, I was restricted. I had allowed others to categorize me, placing me into the tiny boxes of their descriptions. I felt the Lord stirring in my soul, filling my spirit with a song for the world to hear, but every time I opened my mouth, other people's expectations came bursting forth. Fear of judgment, discomfited by other's perceptions of me—I used to hide. My scars were internally hidden from the world, and yet I wore them so close to my heart that I couldn't heal myself and I couldn't accept healing from

God. I would ask myself, *Theresa, who cares that you have a message? All people see is that pretty face; no one knows why you sing.* Until...

July 22, 2007.

My whole world flipped upside down and inside out. Those scars that I had kept so close were put on display for all the world to see. My cells were literally ripped apart and my life stolen from me. When I realized the light was the hospital fluorescents and not the gleam of the pearly gates, I was presented with the question: Who cares? And my answer is, "I am my brother's keeper!"

Who are you?

Job 10:8–14

"Your hands shaped me and made me.
Will you now turn and destroy me?

Remember that you molded me like clay.
Will you now turn me to dust again?

Did you not pour me out like milk
and curdle me like cheese,

clothe me with skin and flesh
and knit me together with bones and sinews?

You gave me life and showed me kindness,
and in your providence watched over my spirit.

But this is what you concealed in your heart,
and I know that this was in your mind:

If I sinned, you would be watching me

and would not let my offense go unpunished."

PART I
MAKING ME IN HIS WAY
JOURNEY TO SELF

1 | JULY 22, 2007

She grabbed me by my hair from behind...

She turned me around to face the full-length mirror.

She cut my throat.

She was behind me; I tried to turn all the way around to ask her, Are you serious? Are we really doing this? A young lady in the bathroom with us ran out, closed the door.

She's coming back... coming down on me again with the... what? I didn't know what she had in her hand, I saw her cut me, but I didn't know with what. She's coming down on me. I raised my left hand to stop her. She's not going to stop. She's coming down now on my face. She's swinging. Everywhere. But my hands are moving, defending. But she doesn't stop. My hands are cut open... my face... I don't feel it, but I see her. She was moving, but she wasn't there. No humanity in her eyes. Vacant. Only the movement of her hands as she cuts, cuts and cuts... across my nose, down my cheek, across my chest, my arm... God, she isn't going to stop. *I turned away from her and slipped, in my own blood. I saw her coming down on me again, and I turned away, exposing my head—her hand, a blade, sliced through scalp. I turned on my knees—she slashed the back of my neck... I turned to my left,* I've got to get up, I've got to get out of here, she's not going to stop! *My baby was there crying, watching.* I have to get this woman off of me, I have to get myself up, get my daughter and then get out of this bathroom, open this door that is now closed! *I was on the door, but she was on me, cutting, slashing, thigh and calf. No one knew that we were down there.*

A sudden push on the door pushed me back, pushed me into this woman, vacant, violent. I call her "my Disobedient Child," the girl who ran out of the bathroom... She's back... my God.

The girl came back with her mother. Her mother didn't know what was going on. All she knew was that someone was hurting me; the girl had not seen the blade. She said, "Someone is hitting on Sister Whitfield downstairs." The girl's mother didn't see the blade either—she saw a hairbrush (praise Jesus for taking away the source of fear!). The mother demanded the attacking woman to "Stop!"

The woman froze. There was no sight, only the whites of her eyes—her pupils were rolled up in the back of her head. "Stop!"

Her irises returned; her face changing, sense seemed to reemerge. The woman ran, out of the bathroom, out the church.

I ran out of the bathroom, forgot my daughter... no, the door was open and I ran out, screaming for someone to get my daughter.

"Something happened to my face, get ice, something has happened to my face, get ice!"

I'm running, thinking I'm alone, but there is a doctor there running with me to the kitchen. I said, "All I need is water and ice, water and ice..." When I asked for ice, ice made me feel better; when I asked for water, water made me feel better; and they were doing all that, and holding me, holding my face together.

I put my hand under the flow of water in the sink; that water splashed over it—my hand opened up like a flower.

Oh no, that's not good, that's not going to work.

I closed my hand immediately. There were others around me—I don't know who—holding me up, holding me together. I said, "Just do the face, y'all just work on the face and I'll keep this hand."

I wasn't scared until I opened my eyes—isn't that something?—all that I'd been through, I wasn't scared, but when I opened my eyes I got scared. When I opened my eyes and looked up at the woman who was holding me, she looked scared and it scared me. Her hair was standing on top of her head, blood was all over her, "Oh my God," there was blood all over the walls, there was blood all over the counter, there was blood everywhere.

Then… the darkness descended on me, the darkness was coming over me… "Whoever is holding me… I'm going."

I felt this… something… I'm feeling something, something is happening… I'm going.

A dark place. I was at a very, very dark place, and I felt the essence of my body leaving me, and I said, "I'm going."

Whoever was holding me, she said, "Okay, you go, I'm going to hold you, I've got you."

With her words something quickened in my spirit, I heard a voice say, "No, you're not. You're not going."

I repeated it out loud. "No, I'm not. I'm not going."

The one holding me whispered to me, "Sister Whitfield, you're getting heavy, I'm going to have to let you go, for a moment."

"It's okay, you let me go. We're just going to hold on, I'm just going to hold on." I held on to the sink, I knelt on it, supporting myself with one toe and an angel's shoulders.

"No, I'm not. I'm not going."

On July 22, 2007, I was attacked in the basement of Trinity Baptist Church during Sunday morning worship service while I had gone to change my then two-year-old daughter's diaper. I was attacked by a young woman named Yolanda Cooper, a member of Trinity Baptist Church, a congregant under my husband's pastorship, a Christian woman, disturbed by a spirit of the devil, possessed in mind, body and soul.

I was saved by God.

God sent his angels to guard me and protect me. The first angel on earth I call my little Disobedient Child—a youth member of Trinity who had abandoned church service in preference to reading a book in the relative quiet of the ladies' bathroom. She was the only witness to Ms. Cooper's initial attack. The girl ran from the bathroom in search of help when Yolanda initially struck me. My second angel on earth was that little girl's mother, "My Little David," who stepped into that bathroom and commanded Ms. Cooper to "Stop!" It was as if she brought Yolanda Cooper back to her senses. Ms. Cooper fled out of the church only to be followed by our deacons until the police were able to catch up with her.

I would not know about the other angels around me until much later.

I was rushed to the hospital in an ambulance. I had asked those congregants gathered around me, holding me together, holding me up, to pray with me before the ambulance came. I feared—I had no prayer for myself but I knew I needed the protection of prayer. I didn't know exactly what had happened, but I had felt my life start to slip away from me. I felt the absence of myself inside my own skin. I heard the prayers of those around me, and I heard a voice inside of me tell me I wasn't going anywhere. My spirit was restored, but my body steadily lost blood out of the over one dozen slashes all over my body.

When the ambulance arrived I must have been somewhat hysterical. I don't like attention, I never have. I could feel the bodies around me, but I didn't know to whom they belonged. My daughter was somewhere but I didn't know where. My other children were not with me that day, and neither was my husband, who had gone to Maryland to a forum about violence in the church. I was in the midst of, the center of, a storm of attention; it made me nervous and I was going into shock. All I can remember is the invasion of an oxygen mask, and thinking, *Are these people crazy? Theresa doesn't do oxygen masks. Don't put anything on my face—my face is already messed up, how are you going to put an oxygen mask on my face?* I was not pleased.

The EMTs comforted me by saying if they put the oxygen mask on, it would calm me; something in me trusted them, so I let them put the oxygen mask on. I liked the way I started to feel, I could identify things in my surroundings, I felt like myself again. The EMTs spoke gently to me, explaining what they were going to do next. They put me on the stretcher, and I told them, "Okay, you're going to do this, but let me tell you about me first"—all of this while I'm bleeding to death. I gave instruction as the paramedics were putting me in the ambulance, "I've got to tell you something, I do not like to ride backwards in an ambulance, I've done it before and I don't like it. I don't like that oxygen mask on my face, and I get motion sickness and I'm claustrophobic." They listened patiently. The last thing I heard was, "My name is Chris and you're going to be okay." I don't remember the ride, I don't remember the sirens, I don't remember the surgery. All I remember is waking up in the recovery room...

Two thousand stitches later.

I remember waking up in the recovery room and hearing voices—nurses coming to me that were not very nice, checking my IV, taking my pulse; they hurt me more than my stitches, they hurt me more than the initial attack.

I was coming in and out of consciousness. They moved me from the recovery room to a room in intensive care, but I don't remember that. I remember waking up in a room with people standing all around me, their hands over their mouths, crying. It was like a movie. You know how in movies one scene goes dark and then you're into another scene—I would close my eyes with one scene around me and open my eyes to find things completely different. I guess it was the medication; I didn't panic, I just floated... in and out of con-sciousness. Until I opened my eyes and I saw my mother.

2 | Wade in the Water

That day was not the first time I'd been attacked. It's merely the attack that has left the most visible scars. My childhood was not idyllic. Many people would not believe having looked at me before July 22, 2007, that I, the pretty light-skinned child with "good" hair and a sweet singing voice, had ever been through anything in my life. But my upbringing was not the stuff of dreams. And being light of hue and soft of hair does not spare you from the darker sides of life's realities.

Life didn't even start out easily. I was born Theresa Stephens on November 24, 1968, in Jamaica, Queens, New York, at Queens General Hospital, premature, my mother having gone into labor after being knocked down a flight of stairs by my father.

There were nine of us: James Henry, Judy, Timmy, Jerry, William, Betty, David, and I was next to the youngest, before my baby sister Vivian. From Timmy down to me, there is only one year's separation between each of us; two years after my birth, Vivian was born.

The youngest siblings, myself included, were called the second generation of the Stephens family. The older children would lament to us young ones, "You have no idea what we went through before you guys came." But what we all went through together was terrible enough. I remember my mother and father were always fighting. Too many times we came home from church and the police were already there. The ups and downs, the fighting associated with alcohol resulted in unspeakable cruelty in our household.

We always hid when my father came home. We knew not to be around because we never knew what we were going to get. He would throw the pipes out of our house, sell the washing machine—just crazy, crazy stuff sometimes. And other times it went far beyond absurd decisions brought on by a drunken stupor. If he'd been on that corner drinking with the boys, then he was definitely coming back raising hell.

I can remember one incident like it was yesterday. My father came home drunk and looking for us. My oldest brothers hid me behind the couch. I don't know where they hid my sisters, but I know Timmy (God rest his soul) hid under the bed. We could hear my father coming through the house like a giant, pipe in his hand. He was looking for all of us and ringing the pipe all through the house, hitting it everywhere. I guess he thought if he made enough noise we'd get scared and come out. But none of us budged; no one came out. I could hear him raging through every room until he got to the bed where Timmy was hiding and he just rang that pipe under that bed. Then he left. Drunk or not, I believe that he knew what he was doing.

When he was long gone, we all came out. Timmy's mouth and face were so busted up, I almost couldn't recognize him. He looked like something from a movie: his lip was open and all his teeth in the front were knocked out. I remember him running around making fun of the way his face was all busted up, until our mother got home. She'd been at the hospital all day, working her shifts as a nurse. She must have been exhausted, but she took one look at her son's face and immediately rushed him to the hospital. The doctors helped, I'm sure, but his face was never the same again.

In remembering my upbringing, the discipline from my mother wouldn't have been called abuse; it was just called raising a child. She truly believed in the Scripture "spare the rod and spoil the child." My mother's temper was quick and all-encompassing, and though she was harsh to all of us, I recall little mercy in my discipline.

She also distrusted me, even when I was a child. I could be sick with a fever and she would insist that I was pretending. Maybe that distrust also played into her rules about friends. Because there was no such thing as friends in the Stephens family. They weren't allowed in the house. You went to church, you went to school and you came home, that was it. You did your chores, you did your homework, you went to bed, that was it. As youth we were extremely isolated from the outside world, and as we all grew into adulthood, each of us took a different path, always straying from the straight and narrow because we didn't know any different.

The perversion of our inheritance from our parents bled into our genes, and what started as a life troubled by alcoholism and anger became a confusing and dark life of shadows for many of us. We all struggled to overcome our individual trials, but too many times we found ourselves struggling against each other. My mother denied the truth of it for years. And I didn't realize, until I was an adult, that there was any other way to grow up.

Before I had children of my own, I just assumed life was lonely and hard and trying, like I deserved the worst for no reason and that was just how it would be. None of my siblings seemed to question it either. Some of them are still too caught up in the lives we lived as children to see that there's more than abuse and violence and pervasion in the world; they can't see past the scars and shadows.

With everything we went through, it only makes sense that we struggled. Physically and mentally we suffered and, in some cases, still suffer. But as a family we still don't talk about that.

We just didn't understand my mother. Especially when it came to her daughters—my mother adored her sons, but we daughters would get together and wonder, "What is wrong with her?" When we were little, we thought she was crazy, just off the chain. It wasn't until I became a woman that I started to really see my mother as a woman, and not just as my mother. Only then could I understand what she had survived.

My mother, born and raised in North Carolina, decided to move to New York for a new start, but she only stumbled into one bad marriage after another. Forty or fifty years ago, times were different. Life was hard and sometimes unbearable—how else could it be when you were trying to raise nine kids on a nurse's salary? She spent our childhoods fearing her own hidden scars and the shadows on her heart—the ones that made her accept abuse in marriage as a necessary evil. A woman had to do what a woman had to do. If it meant sacrificing her own happiness for her children's survival, my mother knew she'd just have to find happiness after we'd been fed.

My mother focused so much on shielding us from a past that tormented her that she couldn't protect us from the abuse and darkness on our own doorstep. She feared we would inherit her scars, and in some ways she was terribly right. None of us came out of the home unscathed. Her scars and her battles are not mine to share, not mine to explain or justify. But knowing her story like I do, knowing her as a grown and married woman myself, knowing her scars through my own, I have found forgiveness in my heart. Now, I can respect that and I can understand.

I may remember many of my early hardships as bad dreams, but I had a lot of nightmares, true nightmares when I was a child. That I can tell you. I always dreamt about the devil, always dreamt about being pulled away. I think I've heard specialists describe dreams like these as growing pains in some psychological study or other. And maybe they had more than a little to do with the reality of my waking hours.

Do you recall, when you were younger, dreaming of something being on top of you always holding you down? Did you lie there, so sure you were really wide-awake? And you couldn't move because something was on top of you? That was my dream. It was ever recurring through my childhood. I'd be in my room, dreaming of the devil and that weight holding me down, and I could see myself just being dragged across the house, and I could do nothing to stop it.

3 | Denying the Flood

Looking back, I cannot and I do not blame my mother for everything that has gone awry in my life. But I know that each of us approaches life based on the foundation that we have been given. My foundation was very strong in some ways. My mother raised nine children. She was a successful professional in a time when blacks were often seen as only domestics or teachers. I attended Carter Community A.M.E. Church, which supported not only my spirituality but also encouraged and cultivated my musical gifts. I received a full education (difficult for me as it was), and along the way, many people came into my life to help. But that foundation was also cracked in some spots.

My preteen and teenage years were difficult for me, both in terms of schooling and socialization. I had trouble with math, and I didn't find help or sympathy at home. I found ways to maintain my grades because it was expected and required, but many a tear was shed over long division. Beyond my mother's expectation that I would bring home good grades, I had little motivation to do well. I wasn't even allowed to take the SATs for college consideration. I understand now that my mother simply didn't have the funds to put us through college, and maybe on some levels didn't understand the process well enough to consider all of the options like grants and scholarships. Her lack of enthusiasm for helping me toward an educated future was simply a matter of funds. Like any other teenager, I had questions about myself to answer. At times, my grades in school would slip because I was preoccupied trying to discover who I was besides my mother's child.

Remember that friends were not allowed at the Stephens home. Instead, I discovered other ways to maintain friendships; but because of a unique blend of naiveté, strong will, creativity, curiosity and anger, sometimes I veered onto dark paths toward relationships that were not healthy. Male-female relationships were limited because I was only so bold about sneaking around behind my mother's back (I didn't understand my mother, but I have always respected her). Still, I experienced enough to know now that it is an easy thing to get into trouble when healthy communication is not part of your upbringing. I was ignorant about the various consequences of physical and emotional intimacy, and I suffered because of it. I didn't see myself as attractive, but the boys liked whatever it was they saw, and maybe I was too easily impressed by this passing interest. And with such a lack of affection at home, it was too impossible to reject the surprising attention of boys who were bold enough to spend time with a "Stephens girl."

I didn't really flourish in school until my senior year, when some fellow classmates overheard me singing one day. I had been singing in church forever, and in grade school I had participated in as many school plays and concerts as my mother would allow (which were not as many as I was asked to be a part of). I remember my glee club teacher picked me out of all the children to sing "The Greatest Love of All" (remember that song?) in our sixth-grade graduation; while rehearsing, people remarked, "Theresa, we can hear your voice all the way through the hallways of the school." But somehow I fumbled through the first three years of high school with no one discovering my talent, and I was not the kind to volunteer.

My senior year, on the other hand, was a whirlwind of plays and musicals. It was an amazing time for me. My classmates swept me into the drama scene of high school. It was an eye-opener, like someone had turned on the lights and I realized what it was I was supposed to do with my life. *Mama, I want to sing!*

An off-Broadway hit had become the truth of my life. It was an odd revelation because I had always sung, and my mother always admitted that I had a true gift, but she never seemed to be able to support me—still to this day I don't understand that reluctance. My mother had little interest in supporting me through a music career, and I would have needed her support.

But what God has for you is for you, no matter what others may do or how the Devil may try to thwart you. I didn't get to pursue a career in music, but I rediscovered my passion for music in that last year of high school. It left me feeling invigorated, excited and confused, especially because I couldn't make sense of how music would fit with the future I expected to have.

The choices for all of us as children were always the same: the military and a job, or the military and college. Really it was one option—the military. I wanted the independence and the freedom of the military, but I didn't want the stifling regimentation of the military. It was no choice at all. I was naturally high-spirited; I wanted something more than what I had. And I think that scared my mother.

I remember walking into the backyard one day to find my mother pinning my sister to the gate; they were fighting, but about what, I didn't know. When I got closer, I shouted, "Why is Mommy beating you like this?"

Sis, still struggling, replied, "Because I won't tell her you're on drugs."

I was incredulous. "I'm on drugs?"

Knowing that I had never touched drugs in my life, Sis said, "Yes, Mommy wants to know why you're always so happy all the time."

I kid you not, my mother was beating my sister because she suspected my high spirit was narcotic-induced. The anger built up in me, and my mother saw it and slapped my face. I wanted to hit her back, and that realization was horrible for me. Before I could lift my hand, I turned and ran. I ran away from home, and I felt I couldn't go back because

I desired to hit my mother.

✦ ✦ ✦   ✦ ✦ ✦

By the time high school graduation came around, I was all of 17, and I was still looking for that light and that hope. That way out.

Turns out sometimes it finds you.

I was working as the floor superintendent at a Roy Rogers restaurant when my way out walked into my life. He looked at me, and I knew things were going to change. Damian was like a beacon of hope for me.

He walked into the restaurant with a group of mentally disabled adults as part of a regular outing from a housing facility where he was a supervisor. His job was to teach them to function in normal society by handling simple tasks like ordering their own food and paying with their own money—which they earned at the facility where they lived. Damian taught them to be independent and successful members of society, and I found his compassion and dedication endearing.

I knew my mother would not allow dating. I'd been through enough just the year before—let alone the rest of my childhood—to know the consequences of making much out of my interest in him. But then came the interruption, the distraction that tempted me before and would tempt me for years to come.

"She's cute," he was saying to himself.

And more than just think it, he acted on it: he gave me his number. I may have been working hard and doing my best to walk a straight line, but I was still 17 and I really l liked him. So I gave him my number, too.

Only when he called my house, I didn't answer. And my mother didn't answer the phone either. I thought that would be the end of it, but no. He came back to the restaurant. Every Tuesday he'd walk in with his people and ask the same questions.

"Why don't you call me? Why don't you pick up the phone when I call you?"

Finally, I gave in and agreed to go on a date. He was to pick me up at my house and meet my mom—but as old school as it was and as nice as it sounded, I knew it wasn't going to fly. And instead of telling my mother—instead of asking permission or talking about it at all—I just hoped he wouldn't show.

When the day came I was getting ready upstairs and my mother was downstairs, with no idea a boy would be driving up in his car to take me out for the evening. I was so nervous I had the jitters. I didn't know what would happen when he arrived, but I was too scared of my mother to walk downstairs and tell her. How could I? It would all have been simpler if he just hadn't shown up.

But he did.

He rang the bell; she answered the door.

I refused to go downstairs. I couldn't bring myself to be a part of it. All I knew was that when I looked out my bedroom window a few minutes later, he was walking toward his car. Finally, my mother's voice rang up the stairs, and I made my way down.

I expected her to slap me around a little—after all, I'd defied her and she was furious.

"Why did this boy think he was going on a date with you?" she asked me.

"Mom, I like him, and I want to go on a date with him!" But pleading would do me no good.

"Do you know what he said when he walked out of here? Do you know what he said about my daughter? When he walked away from this door he said, 'That f'in b! She's never home; she's never around!'" I realized then that she must have told him that I wasn't home. "Something's wrong with that young man. I don't know what it is, but I told him to get away from my door." She waited for it to sink in before she finished. "That is not the man for you."

I think I really should have listened to her.

✦ ✦ ✦   ✦ ✦ ✦

I went to work the next day, and Damian was there with his own version of the story. He swore he would never treat a young girl like that, would never curse out a woman. And I believed him.

Our courtship wasn't traditional. Rather than conquering the mountain that was my mother's strong objection, we just saw each other at the restaurant. He would bring his people there, drop them back off at the center, and return to spend time with me. There were no movies or nice dinners or long walks. Just Roy Rogers and those Double R burgers I still adore.

Like any teenager wrapped up in a secret, my studies faltered. My grades slipped; I stopped working as hard. I brushed off the consequences, too happy in love with Damian. But my mother knew. Her eyes were too sharp to fool, and after years of doing well, she knew I was trying to get away with seeing him behind her back. I fought back, swearing I was in love. Neither of us backed off, and our tempers boiled over. It ended when I left the house for the second time.

It was raining and I had no place to go—no place besides Damian's, anyway. I called him and he took me to his aunt's for a little while until he sorted things out. Eventually, he brought me to his mother, hoping to prove to his family that I would be around for longer than the few days it would take for my mother to cool down. He didn't waste time coming clean with the whole story and with his feelings.

"Mom," he told her, "I want to take care of this young woman."

It was all she needed to give us her blessing. She offered us the little money she had saved for him for whenever he said he wanted to marry. Overjoyed, we got our first apartment and our first car. And it felt like things were starting to work again.

Mind you, we still were not married.

We lived in a basement apartment and paid our bills with two jobs each while we tried to finish school. It wasn't easy by any means, and it wasn't the time or money it took to stay afloat on our own.

We fought every day. He hung out with his boys who smoked, and we argued because I didn't do drugs and wanted him to stop. He would compare me to the older women in his life, and it irritated me. He complained that he had no money now that we were together—forget that we had bills for the first time and were trying to be responsible—and his resentment offended me. Worst of all, we had no trust between us. With everything we had to do, with all the bills there were to pay, we still didn't trust each other.

Despite all the arguing, despite the issues big and small that were beginning to fester between us, we still intended to see it through. We loved each other deeply, and though we never talked about marriage, leaving each other was not an option.

We started talking about getting married the night we found out I was pregnant with my first son, Christopher. When Damian heard, he asked me to marry him. I was shocked. He had no doubts, no reservations it seemed, but my first thought was to say "no."

His mother interceded and had a good talk with me.

It wasn't as if I were making the decision a few nights before. Because I was pregnant, saying "no" meant having the baby out of wedlock.

"I didn't raise my son to father children and not marry their mother," she insisted. And it was true: he saw no other path besides marriage.

I didn't realize that I could say "no," that having a baby out of wedlock wouldn't be the end of me, that I could have at least said "wait a minute" to listen to someone else's opinion. No one had ever explained those things to me, and when it came time to make a decision, I said the only word that I thought I could say: "yes."

4 | Drowned in the Depths

Psalm 51

Have mercy on me, O God,
according to your unfailing love;
according to your great compassion
blot out my transgressions.

Wash away all my iniquity
and cleanse me from my sin.

For I know my transgressions,
and my sin is always before me.

Against you, you only, have I sinned
and done what is evil in your sight;
so you are right in your verdict
and justified when you judge.

Surely I was sinful at birth,
sinful from the time my mother conceived me.

Yet you desired faithfulness even in the womb;
you taught me wisdom in that secret place.

Cleanse me with hyssop, and I will be clean;
wash me, and I will be whiter than snow.

Let me hear joy and gladness;
let the bones you have crushed rejoice.

Six months later, when Christopher was all of three months old, we were married.

At first, we moved in with his family in New Jersey, with his mother, sister, and brother-in-law. And while no family is perfect, their problems quickly intertwined with our problems. We couldn't grow or be ourselves, and we thought that being on our own would help. As soon as we could manage it, we packed up again and moved to an apartment in Edgewater. But that wasn't good enough to stop the fighting.

The trust we'd lacked before didn't magically appear when we signed the marriage license. My early suspicions were confirmed when his friends told me everything he was doing behind my back, and I gave him plenty of reasons not to trust me either. And sometime in the short time between dating and getting married, I realized I'd misjudged him more than slightly. He'd assured me he would never use foul language in front of a woman, and yet he called me every name under the sun when we fought—and we fought every day.

We'd fight so often and so loud and with such fury that the cops were constantly at our house. We even had to settle our domestic disputes in court from time to time, and to this day, the issues that troubled me daily in my twenties linger with me now.

Our marriage progressed at a limp, and by the time Kerry was born two years later, our arguments were turning violent. As if the mental and emotional abuse my first husband doled out wasn't enough, I had to struggle to protect my physical self as well.

It's no wonder I've dismissed so much of my first marriage from my memory. We may have been legally married for fifteen years, but every six months we were separated for one reason or another. Six months in, and the rest of the year out. I didn't know where he lived; I don't know what he did. And every time I believed it was over—finally over. But the people around me could have told you it wasn't. Every time he came back around, they knew we were going to make up and try to start over. It drove our friends away from us because no one wanted to deal with our crazy and toxic patterns. And I, for one, don't blame them.

It took a fall down a flight of stairs for me to realize the truth. He'd kicked me down—so much like the way my father sent my mother falling the day I was born—and when I stood up, I decided that enough was enough. It was the point of no return.

I picked myself up and went back into the house. My boys needed dinner, so I made it like nothing was wrong. But then I looked at my sons—Christopher was five and Kerry was three—and I knew I needed to act. Before we even finished our food, I'd stood them up. I left dinner on the table, I left everything we owned, and we walked out the door.

Someone—at some point—had given me the number for Shelter Our Sisters, an organization that assists victims of domestic violence. When I called, they agreed to meet me at a diner and give us a ride to their facility. Like many domestic violence shelters, their location is as secure and secret as possible, and a ride from an employee is the only way to seek their help. So they picked me and my boys up and carried us to safety.

It was the best thing I could have done for them—and for myself. For six months we were safe.

Shelter Our Sisters required that their residents have attainable goals to continue in the program. Looking at my life, looking at what my babies needed from me, I knew my first priorities were to care for them, and that meant that I needed a good job, I needed a new place to live and I needed to get back into school.

Without the shelter's help, I'd have struggled to reach those goals. They brought us clothes—both outfits for the boys and work attire for me—that hardly seemed worn and that had the smallest of imperfections. We decided what we wanted to eat. If we wanted seafood, there was seafood. If we wanted turkey dinner, there was turkey dinner. The children had all the toys they needed for play, and at night we shared a cozy room and slept without fear. We walked to school together. The kids didn't even know we were in a shelter. That's where their friends were. That's where we laid down our heads. It was beautiful; it was home. *My life began there.*

✢　✢　✢　　　　✢　✢　✢

When the six months were over, Shelter Our Sisters helped me land a good job and helped us get a two-bedroom apartment in Little Ferry. I left the shelter prepared to keep my life on track for once. I had my boys; I had my goals. I had a new beginning and was fueled with the confidence I'd gained at the shelter.

But Damian followed us. How he found us, I can't remember, but once he knew, he kept coming around. And as strong as I thought I was, as much as I knew I shouldn't, I let it all start all over. Before I knew it, he moved in with us and brought back all of the fighting and strife I'd worked so hard to escape.

I'd try to get away again not too much later. At the time we did not have a car in Little Ferry, and there were no buses, and I had to drag my babies through the blizzards. Between the fighting and the hard time I had getting to and from work and the boys' school, I knew I needed to get out. I managed on my own to save up enough for first month's rent and security on a beautiful little apartment in Hackensack all by myself, and the boys and I moved on our own. But again, he came back around and somehow made amends.

It can be hard to explain exactly how you can forgive someone after they've kicked you down a flight of stairs. Looking back, I remember thinking, "This is my husband. This is the father of my children. What else am I supposed to do?"

I had to hope that he would get himself together, that I'd wake up one day to find that things were better. He had potential to be great—in all aspects of his life—but he was struggling to make the right choices. We shared our fears and our goals. We made promises and plans. We'd make love at night, but I'd wake up hating him—deeply hating him—in the morning. No matter what I said or did, no matter how we planned, no matter how vulnerable we made ourselves, it always came back to the same story.

The idea of dating, of getting to know someone all over again and bringing him into my family, was completely foreign to me. How could anyone but Damian help me raise my children? How in the world could I begin to trust someone when the man I'd married all those years ago couldn't even follow through for me?

So I stayed.

✦ ✦ ✦   ✦ ✦ ✦

Sometime after we moved into the apartment in Hackensack, I started going to church. Damian wasn't too pleased—he could see it was making me stronger, more able to take on the mess that was our marriage—but he didn't stop me. We were members of Community Baptist Church at first, but they were growing rapidly and I felt more and more like a number. I wanted to feel like a person, like I could be heard, like I wasn't going to be forgotten as part of the majority. As happening as it was, it just wasn't for me.

Finding my church home didn't happen overnight, though. I'd been singing in an R&B band at a club with a group of musician friends, and a musician from Trinity Baptist Church invited me to come listen to their choir. I appreciated the invitation, but I didn't accept. It wasn't the last invitation to Trinity I'd get, either, but I dug my heels in a bit and never went. Early within the following year during Easter, my sister and I were running late to church, and we arrived at Community Baptist Church only to find it filled to capacity—not a seat left to be had. We then attempted to go to Mount Olive Baptist Church with the same results. Every church we went to was the same way.

Then we passed Trinity. I'd heard about it from so many people that I figured it was as good a chance as any, and we decided to go in. When I stepped into the sanctuary, there were seats everywhere—on Easter Sunday! I was thrilled. Sis and I had a whole row to ourselves, and I felt like maybe, just maybe, I'd found my church.

When the service started, the young pastor took the pulpit and began preaching. I could hardly see him, but it didn't matter. The room could have been completely empty or packed with people—it wouldn't have mattered: all I could hear was the pastor. The longer he spoke, the more his words touched me. And though it made no sense, and though I had no clue what this church was really like or who this man was or what I was thinking, his words made me feel at home at Trinity.

I told myself I had to go back to that church, but a year went by before I had any contact with Trinity again. After an event I attended, the same musician friend that had asked me to visit Trinity the first time asked me to meet his pastor. I shook Pastor Jonathan Whitfield's hand and spoke with him in the parking lot that evening, and that was it. If I had second-guessed myself the first time, I knew this time that Trinity was to be my home church.

I'd spent a lifetime living with the consequences of

anger and hate, so I'm not sure I expected there to be consequences as painful and enduring from love. I was married, but
I don't think there was ever any great love between my husband and me. When I began going to Trinity, I found myself
becoming stronger and stronger each Sunday I attended. My
eyes began to open; though my marriage was legal and bind-
ing, I was finally able to see more clearly the awful, abusive
nature of the relationship I was in. I was a mother of two young
boys, and at some point there would be explaining to do.

Just being there, getting to know Pastor Whitfield as
he preached, interacting with him as my pastor, discovering
this wonderful and exciting feeling that I'd never experienced before—true independence—it was an amazing present that being in the midst of Trinity Church had gifted me.
My head knew better than to think the road ahead would be
easy. I knew there were hurdles to jump—impossible obstacles, they seemed in the early days. I had a lot to do in my
marriage, a lot to take care of in my life. And no matter how
much my heart was drawn back to Trinity every Sunday, I
didn't know how to put these newfound stirrings of independence and self-worth to action.

I wasn't the only one in the equation—I had children
and family to consider. The more time I spent at Trinity, the
more complicated my life became... and the deeper my faith
grew.

Maybe it was my new connection to this church that
made Damian think it was time to go to counseling. We'd
tried once before, with another pastor, but little had come
from it. Our situation was made to sound workable—as if it
wasn't an impossible case and as if we were actually a good
couple. We were given assignments and homework, but we
never went back—and I'm not even sure why. So when
Damian suggested trying counseling with Pastor Whitfield,
there was no reason to think it'd hurt.

Pastor Whitfield's approach with us was much different. It could have been because Damian and I weren't sitting in front of him very long before we were deep into the fighting that we usually reserved for the privacy of our home. It had to have been very obvious that we weren't just a newlywed couple trying to overcome superficial differences. Instead of reassuring us that our world would right itself with hard work and love, he left us with a haunting task.

"You guys need to go home and get to the bottom of it why it is that you really got married."

Neither Damian nor I had any answers, but when we fought we used our insecurities as ammunition. Scars and wounds shared in confidence became rocks to sling at our worst. For years he'd been using the truth about my childhood to pick me apart. Realizing we couldn't even justify why we got married in the first place—much less why we were still together—never became part of that maliciousness, though.

"I don't know why I married you," he'd say. "I didn't mean to marry you."

It wasn't news to me. It wasn't that the truth didn't hurt, but at least he didn't say it with any intent to hurt me. It was simply an admission of the same confusion I felt. Looking back, neither of us knew what we were doing in this messy, dark world. And though Pastor Whitfield's question exposed what was probably at the heart of our trouble, Damian and I never went back.

I met with Pastor Whitfield without Damian once. I'd continued growing in the church and I felt strong enough to have my own counseling—husband or not. In the short time we spoke, I finally came to the firm conclusion that nearly everyone in my life had already agreed with: this marriage was not for me.

The counseling session had solidified a scary truth that I had been running from for a long time. Pastor Whitfield was an amazing source of strength for me once I'd made the realization. He was quick to offer an objective ear, a sound bit of Scripture-based advice and a solid spiritual compass. Over time, the pastor-congregant relationship became friendship. As my pastor, he guided me. As my friend, he comforted me. I sought him out in times of need—and there were many as my marriage grew darker. Our time talking and learning about each other built a friendship like no other in my past, present or future. But sometimes friendship is not enough—the best of friends cannot save us from ourselves.

So much of the fighting between Damian and I relied on using the truth against each other; it only made sense that I would do my best to use it against Damian eventually. My fledgling independence intimidated Damian; he felt the bonds between us starting to slip as I burrowed deeper into my faith. His fury was unmatched. We may have been fighting for almost fifteen years, we may have separated time and time again, but the possibility of me being strong enough to truly live without him was the last straw. I'd insisted I wanted a divorce, that I knew Damian and I were done for good, and he laughed at me.

"You're not going to do anything, you always say this and you never do anything."

And he was right. I had never before pursued it. There were all of five papers to sign to end my marriage, and I had never moved to do it. I was crystal clear in my intent this time, until the results of one tiny test changed the course again. I found out I was pregnant with my third child and first daughter, and my determination to leave him faltered. Could I bring another child into the world and deprive her of her father? As dangerous as it was—mind, body and soul—to stay with Damian, it felt safer than throwing caution to the wind and taking a chance on myself alone. So it turned out he was right. As much as I couldn't be with Damian, there seemed to be no other choice. The threat to divorce him fell empty.

I threw myself back into my marriage, determined to make it work. And I allowed my friendship with the pastor to fall to the wayside. With a beautiful baby girl on the way and an unbearable, mentally abusive marriage, I didn't have the heart to allow myself the hope of his friendship.

✦ ✦ ✦   ✦ ✦ ✦

After our daughter Kellie was born, the world righted itself for a few blessed moments—as it always seemed to do when our children were born. Damian and I had a common goal: provide for our family, enjoy those precious moments that fly past. Like never before, Damian and I managed to get our act together then. We bought a house. We started going to a new church together. Things were so good that I started going back to work when Kellie was old enough for daycare. I started to feel free again, and strong.

But I'd given Damian a villain. He'd been watching for his nemesis to creep back into my life at any moment, and it did—yearning for the peace I had found there, I returned to Trinity and sought counsel with Pastor Whitfield one day, and when I did, Damian knew. He made his mission to subdue me into loving him—into forgetting there was another possibility for my life. But the more he pushed me, the more I pushed back. Our sons had not been enough to keep our marriage healthy, and neither was our daughter. I didn't know how I was going to succeed, but I knew I had to get out of my marriage.

The fighting eventually came to a hilt, and Damian left for what we'd eventually realize would be the last time. After a little while, Damian would come by to see the children, not to make amends. He started moving on and began dating (though to this day he has never remarried or had other children; it just wasn't in his character). It brought me a kind of peace to see him as I'd pictured him in my head, with other women who I knew would suit him far better than I ever had. In *this* peace I finally found the strength to file the divorce papers. He fought it, like he'd fought everything else in our life together. Every delay, every wrench in the machine was from him. Our lives didn't change overnight after the gavel fell. I didn't demand child support, knowing Damian's struggle to keep a job and my steadfast determination to provide for my kids. I didn't force a custody battle, either. I never wanted to keep the children from their father, and after the divorce, Damian would come around and things would be peaceful and nice. We'd smile uncomfortably, unsure of how to be divorced after a lifetime of learning how to be married. He'd eat with the kids, show up on Christmas morning, and hang around just being their daddy.

But it dawned on me one day that he wasn't letting it sink in. To him, nothing had changed except the paperwork. I had to sit him down and tell him like he hadn't been told months before.

"Damian, we're not together. We're divorced. I have to get on with my life."

And after all the years of fighting and hate and horror, it ended in tears. We talked and talked—it was quite something, that conversation—but I made sure it ended with the truth: we so desperately needed to go our separate ways to end the hurt, to stop the pain and begin to heal.

5 | LOOKING BEYOND THE FAULTS

He Saw My Need

ROMANS 8:28 (KING JAMES VERSION)

*"All things works together for the good of them that
love the Lord, who are called according to his purpose."*

My divorce ended a long chapter in my life, but it
was far from being the end of the story. God had a bigger
plan for me. "I know the plans I have for you, plans for you
to prosper" (Jeremiah 29:11). He gave me a taste of joy and
a hint of redemption in the years that followed. He let me
know that my story wouldn't be all about pain and struggle;
He gave me just enough happiness to know that, when He
called and my true test came, I would know He had a bigger,
more glorious plan in mind for me.

✦   ✦   ✦   ✦   ✦   ✦

I didn't immediately seek Pastor Whitfield's counsel;
I think part of me was ashamed that it had taken me so long
to do something that others, including the pastor, had
known was the right thing for me to do. I needed time to lick
my wounds and process what I'd done before I could confide
in anyone, especially the pastor. I had begun to think of our
friendship as special. I allowed a few months to pass before
I called Pastor Whitfield to give him the news.

We had gone a long time without talking again; I
hadn't gone back to Trinity after that last fight with Damian,
and the divorce proceedings had taken some time. It was a
great shock to learn that Pastor Whitfield and his wife were

also in the midst of a divorce. He had been so openly devoted to her when I first started attending the church, but
even good relationships go through bad times. Their relationship had become so terribly public, as all church leaders'
marriages tend to be. And their troubles had become insur-
mountable.

With everything we'd been through—and everything
we'd put the people in our lives through—Pastor Whitfield
and I realized how much we had in common and what a
balm we could be for each other in these times of trial. It was
already clear to me that the friendship I had with the pastor
was special, but I was surprised by how quickly my feelings
had deepened into emotions I had not felt before. In these
unchartered waters, I couldn't have hoped that Pastor Whitfield would feel anywhere near the same way—but he did.
I felt a hope of more kindle between us. As I was learning to
be friends with my ex-husband, I was learning to become
more than friends with a man who gave me hope of being
myself for a lifetime, hope that there was more than bitter
words and hard hands in my future.

We started very slowly. We knew there were many
people who would be affected by our actions, and we
wanted to be as respectful to the situation as possible without cheating ourselves out of the opportunity of a lifetime.
Dating was a whole new world for us. Even though we'd become close confidants at one time, it'd been five years since
we'd really talked, and even then we didn't know each other
the way only two people freely in love can know each other.
It was tough with his schedule. We'd both arrive home, exhausted, and have to push ourselves back out our doors to
make it to the movies or to dinner. Sometimes our only free
time came at one in the morning, but I put my foot down.
We had to court; we had to get to know each other.

And though we both had children and jobs that kept
us going till the last minute of every day, we made time to
talk and enjoy each other. When we talked about the future,

he seemed so sure and so steadfast. In a short time I learned how determined this man was. When he talked about marrying me, he didn't need a ring in hand to guarantee that he'd see it through to fruition.

I knew that moving forward would mean facing the questions and disapproval of his congregation. He sought serious counseling from his senior pastor, but he was resolute in his opinion that our pasts were even more of a reason to stay together. After all, he'd seen me through some of the worst times, and I understood the impact his divorce had on him. And we both believed that we had a future to build together, a future that would prove that the trials we'd been through were not for naught.

When we got married, oh, what a wedding it was! The details of my first wedding should come as no surprise given the struggle I went through in the marriage. I barely had time to do my own makeup amid my rush to get everyone else done up and looking pretty. My hair wasn't done, no one helped me plan, and at the end of the day I realized I'd thrown myself a wedding single-handed, and hadn't enjoyed any of it.

But wedding Jonathan—well, let's just say it left me believing that wedding days are a peek into the future the married couple will have together.

The wedding was held at a church down the street from Trinity, and by the time my limo pulled up in front— carrying me and my $250 hairdo and my MAC makeup—I was nervous. There hadn't been a rehearsal because Pastor Whitfield had planned something with my boys and they begged me to let them surprise me. It'd seemed fine at the time, but sitting in that dress that morning, I wasn't so sure it wouldn't be a disaster. And my sister was late driving in from Pennsylvania. She'd called ahead through the traffic, and we knew we had to wait. On top of everything else, it was the hottest day of the year, and neither the car nor the church had air conditioning.

Finally, my brother came to get me.

"T, don't get upset," he said, trying to soothe me.

"I'm not upset."

"Of course you aren't," he smiled. "You're beautiful."

As we walked into the church, all the ribbons and flowers and bells were just the way I'd wanted them. *Okay*, I think, *this is going well*. We got to the doors, and finally someone whispered instructions to me.

"When they open the doors, you'll have to take a step up. Kerry will be on the other side, ready to walk you toward the altar. When you're halfway down the aisle, Christopher will be waiting to take you the rest of the way."

I was already crying. My sons had conspired to give me away. I couldn't think of anything more perfect for my wedding day. So I told them I was ready, tears and all.

As soon as those big, wide wooden doors swung open, I wanted to change my mind. I felt the *whoosh* of a sanctuary filled to the brim with guests turned toward me. My eyes went wide. There were four pastors at the front, all in their robes and scarves, all waiting for me to start walking.

When you're under the scrutiny of that many people, you realize the truth of why they're watching. At the end of the aisle, I was going to become a pastor's wife. I was walking toward my future as First Lady of Trinity, and many of them were there more because of their role in the church than their role in my life to that point. I suddenly wondered if I was ready for it all, and all I wanted to do was tell everyone I wasn't ready yet.

"Kerry, where'd all these people come from?" I asked in a whisper. "We have to close the door." But I just couldn't step back, and when Kerry held out his arm, I started to make my way down the aisle.

By the time we made it to Christopher, I was crying like a babbling idiot. I was happy and scared all at once. But there was Pastor Whitfield, and I was crying more when I reached him—crying out of love and excitement and nerves and joy all at once. I gave him my best "I love you, oh my God we're doing this" look and he smiled back as if to say, "We're okay. Just get through it."

Each of the pastors had something different to say: one about love, one about Pastor Whitfield, one about me, and finally Pastor Taylor himself spoke about the joining of the families. He put into perspective everything we were doing that day: Pastor Whitfield and I were becoming one in God's eyes, but we were also bringing our children under the same roof. And Pastor Whitfield was accepting me as part of the Trinity family, too.

Then our oldest daughter sang "Amazing Grace," and if there had been a dry eye in the place there wasn't anymore. It was the stuff that made you fall in love with the person next to you. Love just came down and took over the church.

We became a husband and wife. We became a family. And we've been moving forward ever since.

Like our wedding day, our marriage has had its trials, but we've been blessed that they were small compared to the love we have for each other. Our first struggle was really started by that love—and if you have marriage problems that have their roots in love and devotion, you should count yourself lucky.

When you marry a pastor, you understand that he's going to be a busy man, and Pastor Whitfield was no different. He was always on the go, always willing to figure things out on the run, and I wasn't ready for it. And two years in, I realized he hadn't taken time to realize he wasn't single, that

I couldn't read his mind to figure out where he was going or when he'd be home. As devoted to his church as he was, I needed him to be devoted to me, too. At the same time I was realizing what it felt like to *miss* my husband, to need my husband when something was going wrong or right. After fifteen years of my first marriage, I'd never known what love was like. So I needed him to slow down, to talk, to figure out a rhythm we could both handle.

My husband is also the kind of man to encourage you to dream and do or relax and be—whatever it is that will make you happy and fulfilled in life. At first, I found this intense independence terrifying. After fighting for control of my own life for so long, having someone willingly support whatever choice I made was actually scary. I was responsible for myself, in part because he was too busy to be responsible for me. On top of everything, I was getting tired of being a stay-at-home mom. I needed something to do, and more importantly, I needed to feel like I was financially involved in our new family. I have never been one of those women who gets a paycheck and sees new shoes; I'm overjoyed to see my money go to the groceries and school supplies and house repairs. And after being self-sufficient for years, I needed to feel like I was still providing for my children and myself.

What I hadn't realized is that Pastor Whitfield is just as protective of his provider's rights as I am. It took some doing, coming to terms with each other's need to be financially independent. A check from him could solve the problem of not having money in my own bank account, but it wouldn't have made me feel any better about the situation. But we figured it out. Rather than finding work at a desk again, we decided that I could finally pursue a lifelong dream of opening up a daycare in our home.

Things started getting tough when I started working—not with my marriage, mind you, with my life in general. The daycare was great to begin with—six kids in our living room with my older children helping when they could. Leading six children through a curriculum all day is no joke, and we had to expand to part of, then all of the kitchen, and finally the family room got swallowed up, too. Things went well for long enough that I hired someone to help me out.

Then came Kelsey, the glue that holds our whole blended family together. As many knock-down, drag-out fights as we had over how my parenting or his was making their lives miserable, we had just as many amazing moments all thanks to a little baby girl. Our children share a sibling, share blood now. We couldn't have been more blessed.

I seemed to be flourishing on my own. Eventually, my business was so successful that it made perfect sense to get licensed by the state to expand my business and get a real facility. We had developed a greater plan for the day-care: We were going to hire senior citizens to care for the children. My daughter Kellie grew up in a senior-run center; I always admired the discipline and the manners that were instilled in the toddlers at a young age. It was so good for her, and I was ecstatic to have had the resources and the support to put it all together.

But one background check changed that. It turns out that all that trouble I'd been through in my first marriage was enough to strip me of my eligibility for a license. Twelve years had passed, but it didn't matter. The state sent my paperwork back, telling me I was ineligible because of an incident that I had not handle well in the process of my divorce. I was crushed. It ruined my dreams of having a business bigger than a home care service for a handful of children. My poor husband had to help me through the heartbreak. It meant I had to go back to work. My employee needed money, so I gave her permission to run the daycare at my house. From there, everything imploded.

Parents complained that the service wasn't the same. Some left. Others tried to see the trouble through, but in the end there was an ugly power struggle with the woman I hired, and the parents who'd stayed saw the worst as we were closing. In a week it was as if everything was falling apart around me.

Little did I know I'd be attacked in the church bathroom that Sunday.

✦ ✦ ✦   ✦ ✦ ✦

The morning of July 22, 2007, wasn't a good morning. It hadn't even been a good weekend. I was feeling melancholy because I knew Pastor had to go out of town and I didn't want him to go. But he had to leave me; it was his job, after all. Anxiety came over me that morning in the same way it does before I speak or sing: it's almost like I get depressed and overburdened. And I was to be in concert that afternoon, so the night before had been a particularly bad night of mixed emotions. I'd slept all day. I couldn't get myself out of bed. Even the kids could tell something was up, and they just let me read and watch TV. Memories of my husband and I joking around the night before were making it worse.

"You don't have to go to church on Sunday," he'd said as he packed his bags Friday night. "You don't have to go."

"I'm going! I'm going anyway!" I told him.

But as he turned to leave, he stopped.

"Oh, and by the way, Reverend Jordan is bringing Mrs. Jordan this Sunday."

He must have seen the look on my face—the realization that I *did* have to go and that I needed to go and, suddenly, that he wouldn't be there. I put on a good face.

"It'll be fine! *I'll* be fine!"

That night, I called my friend Danine to talk.

"I just don't feel like going to Trinity this Sunday," I complained, "not with my husband out of town."

She had a plan. "You call me tomorrow, and I'll have a whole list of churches to visit."

But did I call her?

Come Sunday, I didn't even bother waking the older children. I just got Kelsey up, put on my white dress and pink heels, and headed out the door.

When I got there, I asked the ushers where they'd sat the guest speaker's wife, and they looked at me like they had no clue what I was talking about. No one even knew she'd arrived!

I set out to find her. She wasn't on the deacon's side or on the opposite side. I finally found her up front, worshiping with her daughter. I slipped in next to them, upset by the whole ordeal, and said hello as best I could. I tried to join in, but my spirit wasn't right. My mind and heart weren't there. And sure enough, the enemy would use that against me.

I felt unnaturally cold; no one else around me was chilled, but I was asking them to turn the air down. Then the music seemed too loud, so I sent a note to the front asking our musician of music to ease up on the volume. But I still couldn't get my mind where it needed to be to worship. Kelsey burst out into a fit in my lap, so I put her down. Not a minute later, an usher was at my side telling me she was pulling the stain off the stained glass. By the time I got there, there was no doubt that her diaper needed to be changed — and the pastor was just stepping up to speak. I hurried downstairs, hoping I'd be back before anyone noticed the First Lady was missing from service.

I passed a young lady on my way down — she was heading down to the basement bathrooms from the direction of the pastor's chair, and I was coming from behind the choir stand.

"Good morning," I said in a rush, passing by quickly.

"Good morning," she returned.

When I pushed the bathroom door open, there were little girls in white everywhere, little angels skipping about before their ministry. They were just beautiful, and for a moment I forgot why I was there. But the smell of a diaper reminded me. So that I didn't disturb the little girls' enjoyment of their preparations, I took the baby into the lavatory instead of changing her in the open.

When my task was done, I stepped out of the stall—diaper held at an arm's length away—to find that the entire bathroom had cleared out save one little girl reading a book. The stark contrast between the scene before me and the one I'd left—bustling with children—struck me as odd. The service was reaching its highest moments upstairs, and the whole building trembled with it.

That's when she grabbed me by my hair from behind...

I was coming in and out of consciousness. They moved me from the recovery room to a room in intensive care, but I don't remember that. I remember waking up in a room with people standing all around me, their hands over their mouths, crying. It was like a movie. You know how in movies one scene goes dark and then you're into another scene—I would close my eyes with one scene around me and open my eyes to find things completely different. I guess it was the medication; I didn't panic, I just floated... in and out of consciousness. Until I opened my eyes and I saw my mother.

I thought I'd died and gone to heaven.

"T, I love you." (I still remember this conversation as if we just had it.) "T, I love you and you're going to be okay." She kissed my forehead.

"Mom," I said, "we have to talk."

She smiled. "When you wake up, I'll be here."

The times I was awake over the next few days, I tried to say everything I could say. I felt so in touch with my inner person because I'd just come through something so terrifying. Some of the truth of it hadn't even sunk in. My husband came in at some point and sat with me. He catered to me and soothed me. Chris came in next to see me. Hoping it would help me relax, he started brushing my hair, but huge clumps started falling out by the handful. We both started to scream.

"What's happening, what's happening, what's happening?" I was in a panic, but when he realized it, he took my hand.

"Mom, you're going to be okay," he said.

As it turns out, I'd been cut so many times, they'd missed a spot on my head and had to stitch that part of me up too.

Finally, at the very end of the second day, Dr. Bikoff came in.

"Mrs. Whitfield, I don't know why you're here today." It was frank and true, and I sensed it down to my core. I couldn't fault him for being honest. "But clearly there was a God there with you. I'm going to show you wounds on four areas of your body that should have killed you. Each one is an inch away from a main artery."

He started with something I could see: "Your left hand. She cut you down to your wrist." The rest I had to imagine. "In the initial attack across your throat, she got you right there—right next to your carotid. That first attack alone should have killed you. From your lips to your ear: there's an artery, a main vein—if she'd even cut a little bit more of your earlobe you'd have bled out. Then there's your chest and thigh…" Every time I look at that scar on my chest, I know God really had to have interrupted something: the scar goes along my collarbone, then skips before continuing across my chest. Really, it should have split me open. My thigh is the same way.

"I don't know why you're here today," he said, "but there must be a reason."

Then he handed me the photos.

"To let you know what this woman did to you."

That's when the tears came. Looking at the blood, the horror… I hardly recognized myself. I'd felt it and lived through it, but looking at it afterwards made me think about it, made me start trying to make heads or tails of it all. The doctor wouldn't let me dwell, though; he had another task ahead.

When I'd finished looking through the pictures, he stood me up and walked me to the bathroom mirror. "Now this is what we've done."

And he showed me.

Little black dots peppered my face where they'd run the sutures. I couldn't see the rest of the stitches, and everyone had been murmuring about my face for so long that it didn't matter. After seeing the pictures, the scars were easy.

"Wow," I said. "That's not so bad."

The doctor was right. God had His reasons. And did He ever have a sense of timing.

Just a few years earlier, I wouldn't have had the strength to come through it. Most of my life, right through the end of my first marriage, I was nowhere near where I needed to be to survive the trauma—emotionally, physically or spiritually. In the short time since Damian and I divorced, I came into my own—and I came into love. What I'd learned about life and myself since marrying Pastor Whitfield was a buoy for my heart. God had given me the love and the family and, most importantly, the strength to survive.

He must have been thinking about the rest of my family, too. The journey was very tough on my husband. In the early days, he was seeking vengeance and questioning God — and no one could blame him. Pastor or not, those feelings are normal. We encouraged him through it, and I put a strong face on for the world when he couldn't bear it. Together we hobbled through, relying on that deep love and those lessons of sharing strength we'd learned just a short time before.

Christopher was almost on his way to college in North Carolina when the attack happened. He was determined to skip his first semester at first, but I put my foot down and he went. It couldn't have been an easy way to start his first few weeks away from home, but he learned to let the Lord help him balance his cares and troubles.

I worried about Jonathan, Jr. I'd seen him take life harder than the rest of us at times; I'd seen him get mad at the world and the trials set before the people he loves. His mother had been sick for a while, and he didn't handle her illness well. So when he saw me down, he wanted vengeance like his father. We did what we could for him. I, for one, just hugged him a lot and let him cry as much as he needed to.

Shadra, our oldest daughter, who always views things from a broader perspective, had a question during her visit with me at the hospital.

"Do you want me to go home and take down the pictures in the house of you and Dad?"

She had me confused there.

"Why, Shadra?" I asked. "Why would you want to do that?"

"Is it going to bother you that you don't look like that any longer?"

"I'm still me, though," I told her. "I still look like that." And then I said it: "If anything, I'm more beautiful."

Whether I realized it then or later, I'd seen my family through the beginning of our recovery and the very beginning of my own.

After a lifetime of cuts and bruises on my soul, after decades of healing just enough to get through the hurt, I was riddled with scars long before July 22, 2007. I'd felt pain inflicted by those I loved and those I detested; those I trusted and those I feared; those I wanted to forgive and those I can only hope to forget. I'd pushed through life to survive, for myself and for my children. And I thought to do that and be the woman I wanted to be, I needed to be everything the world expected of me.

I grew up hearing I was pretty, cute, beautiful, and all it made me want to do was hide the scars I'd been accumulating. I avoided talking about my problems and my pain—remember how quickly I let my first husband run from marriage counseling? How I ran away as a teenager for fear of confronting my mother? I couldn't talk about the truth of my insides to people so focused on my outsides. I didn't feel worthy of the empathy I needed to heal and grow from my troubles. All I could see in myself was a girl people believed too shallow and sheltered to deserve a voice.

But then I looked myself in the mirror one summer day to find that I'd been saved for something. In the blink of an eye, I'd been torn apart and sewn back together for a completely new purpose. And all those scars and sutures looked familiar. My outsides finally looked like my insides, I realized. People who see me know that I've been through *something big,* and they stand less on the ceremony followed around attractive women and rely most on identifying with *me.* They find a way to talk to me. They seek me out to share their stories. And the people who can't handle facing reality— the gossips and the pretenders—they know not to bother with me, because it doesn't get any more real than this.

Even better, God gave me the courage to speak up. For years He'd been telling me that I would reach out to hundreds and hundreds of women, that my writing—not my desk job or my singing—would be the source of my power. But as a young woman, I didn't know how I could possibly minister to people when I didn't know how to relate to them. Even when I became First Lady at Trinity, I didn't understand how I could reach all those people physically or emotionally. But God changed all of that in an instant, and the path from there has been crystal clear.

I may have been brought up to believe that shutting up and being quiet about my business was the only way, but I now know the power of testimony and candor in a community like ours—a community where black women suffer in silence thinking that there's nothing better. I have found that my scars give me the courage to talk about my childhood and my first marriage—as dark as they are. Every woman has been through something that has hurt them, something they don't want to share with the world out of fear or embarrassment or shame. But not every woman tells her story, and too many of us hide in ourselves as if it's just going to go away one day—women of glamour with no face for God. Now I can stand up and tell them that it's okay, that they're not alone, and that God's got more for them than hurt.

Every time I tell someone my story and someone is moved, I set myself a little freer from my past. I'm even setting my mother free. We're all learning exactly how important it is to tell our daughters, sisters and nieces—and even sometimes our mothers—that silence isn't going to make anything better. We're all learning that we can protect ourselves and our children from the terrible legacies of anger and abuse and fear that we always thought were impossible to shake. We *are* better than this. We *are* stronger than this. And, God is great. I will be sharing my story until no one else needs to know that my scars are beautiful.

ISAIAH 41:9-13

"I took you from the ends of the earth,
from its farthest corners I called you.
I said, 'You are my servant';
I have chosen you and have not rejected you.
So do not fear, for I am with you;
do not be dismayed, for I am your God.
I will strengthen you and help you;
I will uphold you with my righteous right hand.

"All who rage against you
will surely be ashamed and disgraced;
those who oppose you
will be as nothing and perish.
Though you search for your enemies,
you will not find them.
Those who wage war against you
will be as nothing at all.
For I am the LORD your God
who takes hold of your right hand
and says to you, 'Do not fear;
I will help you.'"

PART II
CELEBRATE THE SCARS!
EMBRACING THE CALL

6 | At the Well

Sisters with a Thirst

John 16:21-22

"A woman giving birth to a child has pain because her time has come; but when her baby is born she forgets the anguish because of her joy that a child is born into the world. So with you: Now is your time of grief, but I will see you again and you will rejoice, and no one will take away your joy."

This is a message specifically for my sister in Christ, but gentlemen, I think you will take something away from this as well.

Do you remember the story of Jesus at Jacob's well in Sychar, a city in Samaria? He'd just finished a journey and sat at that well because—being human—He was thirsty. The Bible mentions that He was waiting for His disciples to come back from within the city, for they went ahead to get meat, so they could dine together and rest before they continued their journey.

Maybe He was testing the city of Sychar to see if the people would notice Him, for Jesus was a Jew and Jews were not commonly known to come to or close to Sychar, for this city was where all the misfits were—where all the people were who did unorthodox things of which the Jews disapproved: interracial marriages, fornication, drinking, living loudly and living to be seen. It must have been much like the world today—people of all nationalities and all beliefs. Despite how His disciples must have disdained these pagans, these "unclean" people, Jesus insisted on trampling all of the prejudices. And He insisted on waiting at the well alone, all—it seems—to talk to one woman.

The Samaritan woman approached the well at the sixth hour—that's about twelve o'clock, and the common time of the Jewish meal. The day must have been oppressively hot in the scorching noonday sun. But heat or no, it may have been easier for her to get water at the worst time of day. Better to go at noon when she knew she could be alone with her thoughts in a quiet place, where she could ponder and wonder. Easier at noon when she wouldn't have a city's worth of eyes on her.

The woman was focused so much on her situations that they almost blinded her. She could not see Jesus waiting at the well, for her eyes were unseeing even as her mind was focused, and when she finally did see Jesus by the well, it was too late to turn back. She couldn't go around it; she couldn't go through it; she couldn't go above it; she had to come to it face to face. Little did she know that her life would never be the same from that point forward.

It doesn't matter what nationality or denomination you are. You can spend your time focusing so much on negative people and bad experiences that you end up missing opportunities and blocking your blessings. When we're like that, we can't see the future, no matter how bright, because we're still too busy living in the past. And don't think that what you've been through is too dark or too tough for Him to handle.

The Samaritan woman had *five* husbands, and the day she talked to Jesus, she had been with someone else's husband. Without even thinking whether it was right or wrong, ask if it made any sense for her to be with that other man. How many times have you started a relationship on emotional crutches? On the heels of something bad happening? Most of us know we have no business getting involved when there are unresolved issues within us, but we are so afraid of being alone. We're terrified that if we take time to heal, we'll miss out on a good man. So we cover our wounds with tight hair, beautiful clothes and a fake smile, and here in the Scripture you find a woman doing just that. If she were your best friend or your little sister, would you tell her to watch herself? Would you tell her she may need to work a few issues out before finding *someone else* to get involved with? Now be honest: would you tell yourself? No matter how logical we are about it, the need to hide behind our beauty, to use our looks to solve our problems, is a part of us. But it's draining us dry. We don't have to *try* to be beautiful.

For my God and my father called you unto Adam the first man, Eve the first woman. The Bible shows Adam as being created, but God *made* woman. He was the master craftsman as He took this piece of bone and tissue and fashioned it into woman, into you. The woman was God's own special work, if you will. Men, you can't argue with that, for you have come to find out that the woman is the comeliest of all God's creation: pleasing in appearance, attractive and fair. Woman is beautiful by design. God planned and constructed woman to be stunning, and we came out the gate that way. And not only are we beautiful, but we have the nerve to be talented and gifted by God: virtuous women.

During that life-changing conversation at the well, Jesus told the woman all the things she had done and the things she was going to do. He told her how she was beautifully and fearfully made, He encouraged her to put her trust and cares of this world on Him. He commanded her to seek first the kingdom of God and all its glory. He took a moment to teach her some things: how to pray again to her God, whom she knew of only from her forefather Jacob (the Bible lets us know that the Samarians were a misplaced people being brought back to God). Jesus assured her that He was the way, the truth and the light, that no one would come unto the Father but by Him.

When we read this story, we should rejoice that we serve a forgiving and faithful God who still wants us even in our messed-up state. He wants us so much that He sent His son to redeem us. But are you rejoicing? How can you,

you ask, when there's so much in life weighing on you? How can you rejoice when you have to wonder if your man loves you after you've fought? How can you rejoice when you have to think about getting food on the table for your children? When you have to work yourself to the bone so they have more than you did? When you can't find the time or heart to make heads or tails of whatever's in your past, much less love yourself despite it?

Once, Jesus sat thirsty at a well. Now, the tables have been turned; we are at the well waiting and thirsty. We are at His well, women of God, so why are we still thirsty? The Bible tells us that we have all we need to quench that thirst. He says to "give of your first fruits" to honor Him. Too often we give Him an offering of our scraps but not our choice harvest, our pocket money but not our true wealth, our material goods but not our time and attention. He says "seek first His kingdom of heaven and His righteousness," because He will provide for us and our tomorrows. Too often we fit God into our hectic schedules instead of setting our schedules around God. As godly as some are trying to be, we are not being obedient.

Women of God, we are called to be a well for Him. We are the place where the living water gathers, and as His disciples, we are to draw from it and share with those who are lost. We are to show them Jesus, who is waiting at the well to receive us back to His own. Jesus commanded that everyone who has left houses or brothers or sisters or father or mother or wife or children or lands, for His name's sake, shall receive a hundredfold, and inherit everlasting life. He assured the Samaritan woman that God would take care of her, through every day, that the Lord would see her all the way. And it's no different for you. *He will take care of you.* You don't have to succumb to the identities and standards of man. You are more than your body. You are more than your scars.

Your life is orchestrated by God. The Lord knows you and what is best for you, but you have to let Him in. Believe that He has even greater things in store for you and yours. Seek God as never before. Learn to love who He has made you to be. Let go of the silly stuff and grab hold of faith.

Be confident in God and His Word. The words you speak from your mouth determine your outcome. Why not speak good and positive things over your life? You are not defeated; you are a conqueror. "Life and death lies in the power of your own tongue."

7 | OPEN YOUR MIND, ANSWER YOUR CALL

Faith and What You Make of It

1 PETER 4:19

"So then, those who suffer according to God's will should commit themselves to their faithful Creator and continue to do good."

Faith has the power to create and the power to destroy. As Christians, as children of God, we know that there is a deep difference between a life of unbelief and a life of faith. A life of unbelief can be filled with failure, misery and devastation. A life of faith can be joyful, fulfilled and resilient. With faith, you are strong and unconquerable; no one can take your faith from you. With faith, you gain deeper insight into the world around you: "with all thy getting get understanding."

In Genesis 1:26, mankind was given the gift of life, a gift with equal parts opportunity and responsibility. You can't live life to its fullest without living with a purpose beyond your own making. You can exist and say you lived, or you can become something more and spend your days with purpose, in purpose and full of purpose. *That's* living a life to be excited about! In a life of purpose, trials and tribulations can be on every hand, but the Word assures us that every day above ground is a Good Day. Every day we have an opportunity to challenge and strengthen our beliefs and our faith is a Good Day. We were created to have life and to have it more abundantly, with everything God promised us and envisioned for our lives. But living with such faith, being His well for the thirsty, is by no means easy.

The words Jesus spoke at the well are meant to give us courage on our journey through life. The challenges we face, the experiences that force us to grow are intended to be temporary scenes played out on the stage of our lives of continuing peace and happiness. Yes, sadness will come, as will heartache and disappointment. Trials and hardship are inevitable events in life. But they are not intended to be the *substance* of life.

I do not minimize how hard some of these events can be, how much they may have weighed upon you even up till this very day. But the lesson Jesus teaches us is very important: trials can extend over a long period of time, but they should not be allowed to become the confining focus of everything we do. Our lives can and should be wondrously rewarding. God's laws give our life glorious purpose as we conquer and ascend past the difficulties of life. This perspective keeps challenges confined to their proper place and gives us a constant guide for action.

But having a plan doesn't mean that the pain, hurt, anger and disappointments are gone. Many of us need to know why—why life turned out this way, why you can't shake your burden, why God has given you the path that's yours. How many times have you asked, "Why me?"

Have you ever sat down to think about how many times you've asked the Lord to bless you, to change something, to make you better? Were you serious when you asked?

If you answered "Yes," then you have had the bold audacity to put your own will second to His, and turning away from *your* own will is not an easy thing.

If you're really serious, you're giving God the go-ahead to do what needs to be done. You're asking Him to make you over, and to do that, God has to break you first. He's got to shatter you into a million pieces. He's got to squish you down into the clay you came from, put you into His hand, and form you all over again. If you're still asking,

"Why me," maybe you need to look at those scars of yours and think about the person He's making out of you.

✦　✦　✦　　　　　✦　✦　✦

What You Really Need

ECCLESIASTES 2:10-11

I denied myself nothing my eyes desired;
I refused my heart no pleasure.
My heart took delight in all my labor,
and this was the reward for all my toil.
Yet when I surveyed all that my hands had done
and what I had toiled to achieve,
everything was meaningless, a chasing after the
wind;
nothing was gained under the sun.

Being created in the image of God is not a state or condition, but a movement with a goal, a purpose. In a familiar prayer, St. Augustine speaks of human life as ever on the move: "You have made us toward yourself, and our hearts are restless until they rest in you." As seeking and restless beings, we are always searching for the fulfillment of a life not yet realized. That thing ever beyond our reach is a need, and we are unsatisfied unless we're working toward those ever-elusive goals.

Animals have needs, too. But they're simple. When an animal is hungry, it eats. When an animal is tired, it sleeps. Their needs are predictable and triggered by survival instinct. Humans, on the other hand, are dynamic in every way. We have a surplus of drives and needs. We want for things we don't need. We want for things we can't have. And no matter what things we possess, we are still unsatisfied. Our restless hearts prod us forward blindly, and though worldly goals never bring us peace, there is a path to deeper satisfaction. Finding fulfillment means being open to a future that we cannot envision on our own. We desire to be in the know, but the only way we will be satisfied, the only way we will find rest, is to answer The Call. So long as we can hear the call above the din of our daily lives, that is.

Can you remember who and where you were ten, fifteen years ago? You were probably all over the place, trying to land on something solid. Maybe you were running haphazard through life, trying not to trip over messes you made with half-promises and sorry commitments. I know I was. Maybe you're getting better, promising yourself that this time you'll do it right... okay, *next* time you'll do it right. Or maybe you're still in the thick of it and searching for a way out. No matter where you are on that mountain of self-defeat, *today* is your day.

Today you're going to take a stand in your faith. Today you're going to decide that enough is enough.

The next time you walk out your door, you'll know exactly how to get yourself out of the mess you're rushing into.

You've got to look to God and give up the empty roots of needing—because with God in your life, those little wants and desires are going to seem far less important.

When things are getting out of hand, just remember:

You don't need to know the future when you're rooted in the Word of God. There's no reason to get frustrated or to throw in the towel because you don't understand; God's in control!

You don't need romantic drama when you have the Passion of Christ. You don't need the trappings of false desire or empty lust.

You don't need the distractions, drama, worry or pain, when the love of God will fill you and sustain you if you let Him in.

You don't need nagging when you could be praising. Negative people weigh on our souls, but giving honor and glory to the Lord lifts the Spirit. Be in the moment of praise and resist the nagging voices, even if they are your own.

You don't need to be out of the moment. When you are fasting and praying to honor the Lord, you don't need to be wondering about your next meeting or personal encounter. Be with God in His moment, and He will be with you in yours.

When you remember you've got power—through Him—to put aside the needs and wants driving you into the darkness, remind yourself of the things that you do need:

You need the peace of Jesus.

You need a clean heart.

You need the prosperity of the Spirit.

You need to live an upright life.

You need your children to walk in the way of God.

You need to cleave to your spouse.

You need to bless the Lord at all times.

You need your relationship with God.

Act on your true needs every day, and when your old restless spirit itches for something more, turn to God. Praise Him. Pray to Him. Seek His Word. Before long, that mess will clear away, and your seeking heart will find what it's really been looking for: purpose through Him.

✦   ✦   ✦   ✦   ✦   ✦

Purpose

ROMANS 8:28

"And we know that in all things God works for the good of those who love Him, who have been called according to His purpose."

I'm challenging you to live with purpose, in purpose and on purpose because we serve a purposeful God.

He created you *on purpose*. It's not a mistake that you are on this Earth. You are a gift to mankind just waiting to find an outlet for all the meaning and purpose He has given you.

Because it is gone, we call yesterday the past. No matter where you've been, how much you've been through and how you managed to survive, your purpose is not in the past. Tomorrow isn't your purpose either; God has the future well in hand, so you don't need to worry over it. Today, though: you are *here* today. Today is God's gift to you — that's why it's called the present. Today is packed full of exactly what God intended for you. Making the most of this gift, though, is up to you.

It's All About Perspective. The approach you take to shouldering an action is as important as the time you spend on the task. Whether you realize it or not, you've already decided whether or not you *believe* you'll succeed.

Optimistic people see themselves as up to the challenge ahead, as greater than the task put forth. Better yet, an optimistic person with faith believes him or herself up to *any* test: "I can do all this through Him who gives me strength" (Philippians 4:13).

If you take a pessimistic view, however, you can think yourself right out of a God-purposeful opportunity.

Pessimists believe they have been defeated before they even begin. They lose sight of God's promise to walk with us even in times of trouble, and they cannot forgive themselves when they fall short.

You can *think* your way right into failure.

Pessimism is not of God. Your thoughts and attitudes serve as conduits for the divine energy you need to take on a godly purpose. Fill your head with self-doubt, and you'll stifle everything you need to serve Him. Man must believe he is capable "for as he thinks within himself, so he is" (Proverbs 23:7a). The song "The Solid Rock" reminds us: "hope is built on nothing less than Jesus' blood and right-eousness." If you lose hope, you lose the strength He can bring you when you need it most.

Think hard about what kind of person you are. Are you an optimist, full of faith in yourself and, more impor-tantly, in the God fueling the divine fire inside you? Or are you a pessimist, denying yourself the means to succeed? Norman Cousins, journalist and author, once said, "The enemy is a man (or woman) who not only believes in his own helplessness, but actually worships it… He is an enemy because of the proximity of helplessness to hopelessness." If you are a pessimist and failing, the greatest enemy you'll face on your road to purpose is yourself.

Realism for the Faithful. You may have developed limited beliefs about who you are and what you are capable of because you honestly believe you will never succeed. Too many people forget to retreat to God for reassurance and strength, and instead drown in the quicksand of reality.

Realism causes a few problems when you try to com-bine it with faith. Believing that a baby was born by a virgin is not realistic. Believing that a man can make the blind see, the deaf hear and the dead live again—that's not realistic ei-ther. Believing in a God who knows you, from your first breath to your last thought, who cares about every imaginable aspect of your well-being even though you've never seen His face, isn't realistic. Being realistic is having faith in something that's been demonstrated before, in something you can prove exists. But then, that's not really *having faith*, is it?

The great leaders and destiny seekers of our world aren't realistic. They're impractical and headstrong and forever shock us with their decisions. Great leaders think outside the box and defy normalcy. There's a reason we prize their differences. They succeed not because of their own innovative spirit, but because God told us long ago to expect the unexpected: "But God chose the foolish things of the world to shame the wise; God chose the weak things of the world to shame the strong" (1 Corinthians 1:27).

Leave realism to the people who don't have a wonderful God guiding them to do great things in His name. Give Him your faith and prepare yourself for a life of *unrealistic* purpose, because He'll never cease to surprise you.

A Purpose for Hope. You've seen how important it is to steer clear of negative mindsets. If you're going to pursue a godly purpose, you need to be an optimist, and you need to let that optimism carry you through even your darkest of hours. Jesus set the example in His own time of mourning. When His dear friend Lazarus of Bethany fell ill, Jesus turned to the hope of His Father. He said, "This sickness will not end in death. No, it is for God's glory so that God's Son may be glorified through it" (John 11:4). Even when He heard Lazarus had died, Jesus spoke words of comfort to Lazarus's sister Martha and to Himself. "I am the resurrection and the life," He reassured her. "The one who believes in me will live, even though they die; and whoever lives by believing in me will never die" (John 11:25-26). Jesus wept at this man's grave but sought hope instead of giving in to despair. He trusted so deeply in His Father's power and grace that even a friend's death couldn't shake his purpose.

It's one thing to look at one person's path and hold out hope; it's another to remain optimistic as you travel your own. Even Jesus struggled with this. He knew His purpose on this Earth. He knew why He was human and why His mortality would change *everything*. But in the moments before He took His final steps toward His destiny, Jesus was afraid. He was so afraid that He prayed that it be God's will for His destiny to change. But He knew that His purpose was for Him alone—no one else could fulfill it if Jesus backed out, and God didn't offer Jesus a second path or a back-up plan. Jesus was the only person who could die on the cross and be resurrected. Death itself wasn't even the hardest part about Jesus' destiny! Everyone dies, but the resurrection, the rising from the dead, the sacrifice for a world of sin: that alone was Jesus' task. He knew succeeding meant He would rest in eternal life with his Father. Can you imagine that Jesus would have carried the cross if He *doubted* His purpose?

Yours and Yours Alone. Part of your challenge and part of your joy should be in the individuality of your purpose. You cannot and shall not live another person's destiny, for what God has for you is for *you*. Not your neighbor or your child or even your twin. That illness that he healed you from was for you. The drug addiction you were delivered from was for you. The lying, stealing spirit you're fighting: yours alone. But so was that moment of peace you found yesterday; that was only yours. What is for you is for you: the bad, the different and even the ugly, but also the good, the empowering and the awe-inspiring. Eternal life might be ahead for all of His faithful, but your road and your reward are personalized.

All of these things make up you and your life, which is a testimony for everyone that you touch. Next time you find yourself wishing your hardships on someone else or praying for that blessing your neighbor found, remember this: "What's for me is for me. Even the me that is me is for me." Repeat that every day. You can try as hard as you want to ride on someone else's dreams, prophecies, desires and passions, but you're not going to get anywhere. Instead, tap into and exercise the gifts God has given you; it's the only way you'll ever begin to understand the power He can have to change you for good.

Fresh Faith, Budding Purpose. Jesus lived a life of faith. Optimistic people, like Jesus, produce faith by inspiring others to see the good. They can start to accept God's hand in their daily lives, and with a light heart, learn not to be afraid of taking opportunities. If you believe the best of God, His plan, and the gifts He's given you, you'll start to be a well of faith for the thirsty—just as He's asked you to be—with purpose.

✤ ✤ ✤ ✤ ✤ ✤

Make the Shift toward Your Destiny

It is for you to see you have a need, and to take that need to God. But it's also for you to separate your needs from your wants. In Philippians 4:19, we're reminded that "God will meet all your needs according to the riches of His glory in Christ Jesus." Notice there's nothing in there about your wishes or desires. Learning to prioritize is key in accepting God's will for your life. Your priorities determine your attitude, your actions and ultimately your ability to make the changes necessary to shift toward your godly purpose.

What's in a Word? The words you speak and think have great power over your mind. Every morning when you wake up, you start grilling yourself with questions—even ones you don't ever expect to have answered:

How come I have to get up right now?

Why aren't there more hours in a night?

What if I hit the snooze alarm just one more time?

Could I afford to just stay in bed today?

Do I really have to start another day like this?

And as you get in the shower, what are you asking yourself?

Why do I have to go to work?

How bad is the traffic going to be today?

What kind of stuff is going to be dumped on my desk today?

Did I forget to finish something yesterday? Will I hear it when I get in this morning?

Can I actually get everything done today?

Isn't there something I'm forgetting? What if it's important?

If you drown yourself in negative questions every morning, how can you awaken with a spirit of optimism, a readiness to grasp godly opportunity when it presents itself? What if, every day, you started by asking questions that would put you a positive frame of mind?

Tomorrow morning, start your day off with the following questions:

How will God change me for the better today?

How can I use my day to improve my quality of life?

How can I use today to work toward my destiny?

What can I improve in myself today?

How can God use me in this world today?

These kinds of thoughts will help you remember to be grateful, happy and excited about being saved. When you chose to spend your first waking moments meditating on God's purpose for you, you're truly waking up *with your mind*.

When you start to get ready, tell yourself, "I woke up this morning with Jesus on my mind!"

Brush your teeth and remind yourself, "God has a plan for me."

Get in the shower and think, "This new day is a blessing for me to use for His will."

While you're shaving or drying your hair, look at yourself in the mirror and say, "I'm beautifully and wonderfully made for a purpose that is mine and mine alone."

If you really want to shift toward your destiny, you need to harness the power of your own words and task them to lifting your spirits and preparing yourself for the day. Make that shift part of your daily routine, giving yourself consistent reminders that you don't need to worry or settle for realistic outcomes: you've got a great God on your side.

A Shift in Words. Beginning to live with the purpose He's given you is all about shifting, changing from one thing to another. In cars we have gears that we shift in and out, whether you are consciously aware of this or not. Automatic or stick shift, every car's gears operate in the same manner. In order to get from one destination to the other, the gears need to shift in order to change speed. There needs to be enough gas sent through the engine to support the speed and to move those gears. In every shift you are picking up speed, getting the power you need for the change. This is as true for your spirit as it is for a car engine. With every decision you make, with every conviction you hold close, you are shifting toward your destiny.

So what's your destiny? You may already know; God may have already shown you the answer. If you're still looking, there's only one place you'll find it. The Greek word for destiny is *rhema*. Literally, it means "utterance." But we faithful use it to explain something so much more complicated and powerful: it's God's spoken Word, and it can change any situation and reveal His purpose for your life.

Even if you didn't before, you now know the effect your own words can have on your life. When you're at the precipice, desiring to change or push toward your destiny, you need to consciously select your words. Words shape your beliefs and impact your actions. Think of your words as your gears for shifting toward your destiny. Words are the fabric from which all of your questions and statements and thoughts are cut.

Be precise in the words you use, for they carry meaning. Your words have something to say to you about your own experiences, but they also have power over others. Have you ever been dissatisfied or upset over a conversation you had with someone? Take a close look at the words you were both using. Words can produce illness; words can kill and destroy. Words can also heal; words can soothe and praise. And when it comes time to shift, you'll need to know what words to use. By changing one word in a question, you can instantly change the answer you'll get; and when you're speaking out for your godly purpose, the stakes are high. Your words have power. Choose them carefully.

Thankfully, our paths are lighted by *rhema*: "In the beginning was the Word, and the Word was with God, and the Word was God" (John 1:1). Get to know His words for your life: the good and bad words, the depowering and empowering words. All words of the Bible are for you to select and use to encourage, to build up, to repair, to strengthen and sometimes to weaken, and to enlighten. Donald Lawrence's song says it best: "Speak over yourself / Encourage yourself in the Lord." Use these words for yourself. Use them for your families. Use them for your enemies. Use them when you don't know where else to turn. All of the words we need in life are in the Word of God for us. The Word of God framed this world from its very beginnings, and it will frame you as you shift.

The Power of Honesty. Consistency is the key when you're training yourself to start your day with positive, God-focused thinking. At some point you have got to stop thinking and start doing. You must now become a doer of the Word, not just a listener. And whether it's the beginning or the end of the day, honesty is the key when you are starting to walk with God. You want real results—you have to get real with yourself. This starts by evaluating your progress. Ask yourself:

How did I progress today?

What have I given today?

What did I learn today?

How did God use me today?

With persistence of positive thought and follow-through actions, you may become proud of your answers to these self-evaluative questions. But don't get caught up in self-congratulations. Pride is a sin to be wary of because the temptation feels so good. Remember, there is always room for improvement.

And when you fall short, which you will (we all do), take care to give yourself constructive criticism and lecture in love. Paul recognized that we will never see our purpose completely fulfilled on this earth: "But one thing I do: Forgetting what is behind and straining toward what is ahead, I press on toward the goal to win the prize for which God has called me heavenward in Christ Jesus" (Philippians 3:13-14).

Ask yourself these questions every day, and trust your gut response:

Who am I?

Why am I here?

What am I really doing with my life?

What am I committed to?

What makes me happy?

What in my life is holding me back?

You may have found many places, trying to find the answers to those questions. (You are now reading this book.) But there is no guide more telling than your own conscience. Listen to your inner voice. The whisper that reminds you what's important. Let that inner voice guide you closer to God, closer to the things that matter, and further from anything weighing on you.

Be true to yourself and honest in your words.

✤　✤　✤　　　　✤　✤　✤

A Study of Powerful Words

This whole chapter has focused on two words essential to a godly life: purpose and destiny. We use these words often enough that they might seem ordinary and commonplace, but they have the power to quicken your spirit if you let them. In fact, these words are so powerful they've started something in people's lives across the ages. You can look up their definitions in a dictionary and get a good grip on their meaning; but when you open the Good Book, you will find a whole new level of understanding. I'd like to share my study of these words with you.

Purpose. On its face, there doesn't seem to be much to this word. English teachers will tell you it means a reason something exists, that having purpose means you have a clear goal. Businesses and college students all write out "purpose statements" by which their actions are to be judged. Children use the phrase "on purpose" to accuse each other of mischief made with intention. Not too long ago, Rick Warren of Saddleback Church took the country by storm with his inspirational books about *The Purpose Driven Life*. His version is closest to the one you'll find in Scripture, but so few of us took the time to investigate it that we may have missed the deeper implications for our lives.

You know that we serve a God of purpose, that He has a goal in mind. God was up to something when He created us, something greater than what we see and say every day. And if God created us with a purpose, we should be people of purpose, people with an aim, a goal to direct our daily lives.

Remember what Paul said in Philippians 3:14: "I press on toward the goal to win the prize for which God has called me heavenward in Christ Jesus." His goal was his call forward, his invitation from God to come a little higher, for the prize is so beautiful and glorious. He had one aim, one purpose: "Forgetting what is behind and straining toward what is ahead" (Philippians 3:13).

Look to Paul's revelation when you're answering God's call for your life. Forget the past and look to God's future. Remember that *today* is your gift from God. No matter how tough the path is, no matter how dark the days, God's got something great in store for you: "And we know that in all things God works for the good of those who love Him, who have been called according to His purpose" (Romans 8:28). When you're moving in God's purpose, you'll see the crown of victory, and Jesus the Christ beckoning to you and encouraging you to hang in there. For it ain't over until God says it's over.

Destiny. Destiny seekers abound. How many characters in books, movies and TV talk about their destiny? Destiny seems to be a recurring theme for superheroes, and for good reason. Destiny is a course of events arranged for one being by a superhuman power.

When you think of superhuman, super*hero* seems to fit just right with a destiny. So do all of those epic warriors and tragic heroines who take one last stand to save a nation or who sacrifice something they love for the greater good. When we hear that *they* can't change their destinies, it's simply a plot twist that keeps us interested.

In real life, there is a superhuman power in control of the course of events, and He's been in control since before He breathed life into Adam and Eve. A superhuman just has powers and abilities greater than humans, and God certainly fits the bill!

The meaning of "destiny" clearly indicates that it's not something that man can bring you. A man can inspire you to have a goal. That goal can even require you to do great good, be emotionally rewarding, take a lifetime to achieve and fit within all of the laws and edicts of Scripture. These goals, though, can never be your *destiny*. The course of your life is orchestrated by God, and God alone.

Ask yourself these questions, and be prepared to be completely honest with yourself—life or death lies in the power of your own tongue:

Are you seeking God's destiny for you?

What actions are you taking toward your destiny?

If you think too much about what *you* think your destiny should be, you'll distract yourself till the end of time. Some people believe that our destinies are based on the decisions we make and the actions we take—but they forget that we've already been created for a purpose and our actions can't change that. Some believe that what we get is what we deserve—but those people are stuck living for the past and its successes and failures. Some people believe they've made so many bad and unconscious decisions that when bad things happen, they think their destinies are cumulative results of all of these bad decisions. All these people have forgotten the meaning of *destiny*.

Pray over your call to purpose and seek answers about your destiny only in God and His word. Have faith that the things you do not know and cannot comprehend are well in hand with our benevolent Father in heaven. Long ago He gave us a promise that should forever remind us that a life of faith in Him is far beyond our understanding—and more joyful than we can imagine: "'For I know the plans I have for you,' declares the Lord, 'plans to prosper you and not to harm you, plans to give you hope and a future'" (Jeremiah 29:11).

✦ ✦ ✦   ✦ ✦ ✦

Answering with Conviction

We've determined in answering His call to purpose we will see and experience all things, whether they're good, bad or ugly. All of these things are considered lessons for our growth, and in all of these things He has a plan for our greater good. That means He's got a plan through all of our afflictions and trials. Through all of the persecution and calamities to which we are exposed. Through all the things that teach us about our frail and dying condition, things that show us that we are only here on His earth for a season. In all things so trying and painful they lead us to cry out, "Oh, my God," but also in all things that remind us that heaven is our final home! In all things that give us joy, and in all things that heal our wounds. In all things that leave us scarred and broken, and in all things that rebuild us afterward. *In all of those things, God works for your good because He loves you and because you have been called according to His purpose.*

The stories of our forefathers—Abel, Noah and Abraham, and their sons and grandsons—are remembered in Hebrews 11, because no matter these men's trials and pain, they lived *by faith* and lived to know rewards that outstripped their afflictions. They answered their calls, offered themselves up as vessels of His will, and spent their many lifetimes changing the course of history in the most unlikely and unrealistic ways. If you answer your call to purpose, you are deciding to live *by faith* with the same conviction in your heart and mind as Isaac and Joseph and Moses. To reach your destiny, though, you must be converted into the tool God needs you to be.

As God is the only one who can mold your destiny, so is He the only one who can mold you for it. God does not convert us without design, and his designs are not new: they are eternal. What He allows to happen to you and what He does with you, He always meant to do. He's already put part of His plan for you into action, by assuring your salvation and the eternal rest as He has for all of His people. As prepared as He is for you, though, you may not be prepared for Him.

You may have seen how He's shaped a few of His faithful before. Abraham was told to sacrifice his beloved son. Job lost everything. Jesus was crucified. I count myself lucky to have my scars when so many have lost so much more. But He won't always wait for you to be ready for the call; He won't give you warning about the lessons He needs you to learn before you're His through and through again. And ultimately, He's going to ask and give you the choice to let Him into your life 100%. You've got to get yourself ready to say YES.

As you stand at the crossroads between the wilderness and your destiny, you'll know what Jesus knew at the Last Supper: "Jesus knew that the Father had put all things under his power, and that he had come from God and was returning to God" (John 13:3). Jesus knew He had been given all things, and He stayed humbled; He knew that what looked bad about His immediate future was eventually for His (and our) good. He knew that He had come from God and would return to God. He believed that all things, all of the events orchestrated in His life by God, were for Him. But even Jesus had to make a decision as He taught us how to pray for God's will to be done in His life. He had to make a decision to lose the things of this world in order to fulfill God's destiny for His life.

He satisfied the Scriptures and secured our salvation. For He came to earth as a child. He suffered, misunderstood by His parents, rejected by His own people, harshly criticized by the Pharisees and deserted by His own disciples. Then on the cross, He suffered for a crime He did not commit. He was an innocent man taking the place of guilty men and women. Jesus decided. He committed, even as He prayed for a change in His destiny, even when He could have turned from God and His people. He succeeded in fulfilling His destiny to gain for us all an eternal resting place with our Lord.

Now because salvation has been secured and because Jesus satisfied the Scriptures, we can sing the hymn written: "There is a fountain filled with blood drawn from Emmanuel's veins; and sinners plunged beneath that flood lose all their guilty stains." Now we can look at our own situations and claim the victory, for the great battle is already won! Can you claim that victory in your own life?

Do not dismay whatever betides: God will take care of you. That promise is in His Word. He promised He would never leave you or forsake you. He is calling you forever forward, always to strive a little higher so that you commit to succeed and to answer the high calling, which is from Him.

What do you believe?

Bless the word of the Lord.

For His word is already blessed for our destiny.

8 | SEEKING FORGIVENESS AND HEALING FROM OUR GOD OF PURPOSE

No matter where you are in your journey with God—whether you just arrived to His well, committed boldly to His purpose for you or are somewhere in between—there will always be times when you must look at yourself and come to terms with what you see. You will have to investigate your scars, to clean the wounds on your soul, to open yourself up wholly. But are you ready to answer the question He's going to ask you? "Who are you?"

Whether you're standing before Him to atone for a sin or beg for His healing grace, He'll ask. For those seeking forgiveness, He wants to see your humility and your honesty. For those seeking solace, He wants to know you trust His aid enough to bare even your deepest wound. With faith that God always has your best at heart, trusting Him completely is your best hope for regaining your strength—both worldly and spiritual.

One lesson in soul-searching is a passage of Scripture from the Old Testament: Psalm 51. The text must be read carefully in order to hear how the writer of this psalm articulates his relationship with God. If you read the text on that deep level, you may gain some insight into how God deals with us as people—no matter what answer we find inside ourselves to give Him.

The Backstory. This man's story really begins in the book of Samuel, and you may even know this man well. The book of Samuel tells us that God chose this young shepherd boy, named David, to be king of Israel because he was "a man after his own heart" (1 Samuel 13:14). The Bible follows David's story closely. God protected and helped David throughout his life. David killed Goliath the giant because God was with him. He assembled a band of men and became a hero leading raids against the Philistines because God was with him. The books of Samuel record victory after victory that God helped David and his men achieve. David became king of Israel, the anointed one of God. David was God's man of the hour, and because of David's faithfulness, God promised that his descendants would always rule over Israel.

We humans are very good at hearing the success in a story, seeing all of the right, picking out the good things. And we are quick to congratulate ourselves, to say, "I'm not really so bad. " After all of his successes, David could have prayed the same prayer as the Pharisee in Luke 18:11: "God, I thank you that I am not like other [sinful] people! " But— as many of us have been and will be in our lifetimes—David found himself in a situation where the evidence of his sin was too obvious to ignore: he had taken Bathsheba. He had killed her husband, Uriah the Hittite, in order to steal her for his own. And now Nathan the prophet had confronted David for what he had done because David could not hide any longer from the truth. He had to face who he was.

A Reading of Psalm 51. The psalm's superscription tells us that David offered the chapter as a prayer to God in his moment of greatest shame. That it's a prayer isn't un-usual—most psalms in the Psalter are. This psalm is not a standard morning prayer: "Lord, forgive me for anything I have done that is wrong." No. Psalm 51's first two verses are an open confessional to God:

> *Have mercy on me, O God,*
> *according to your unfailing love;*
> *according to your great compassion*
> *blot out my transgressions.*
> *Wash away all my iniquity*
> *and cleanse me from my sin.*

Now remember, this is David's first response to the accusation of his sin. He admits, "I am that man who broke your laws. It is I. It's not my mother; not my father. It's me, Lord, standing in the need of prayer."

Notice that the confession is first a confession about God. We can only come before God from such a fallen place in life if we acknowledge His mercy and grace; we must acknowledge that everything that is to follow depends not on ourselves and our abilities, but on God and His grace. The psalmist comes before God with a sense of commitment to God and a profound sense of contrition.

To begin with this type of prayer means that you understand you are a sinner before a holy God. There is no false piety, no excuses made for the sin. You understand that the only way out of this sin is an act of mercy from a gracious and a forgiving God. The cry "Have mercy on me" strips away any pretense to self-righteousness or personal merit.

In the next three verses, the psalmist moves into even more direct petition. Verse three offers:

> *For I know my transgressions,*
> *and my sin is always before me.*

Again, David acknowledges his sin. Many of these psalms were prayed in the temple before the community, so David's may even have been a public confession. Just because David may have confessed aloud doesn't mean you must always bear your soul to the public. But when you have done the things that David did, the private matter becomes a very public affair.

David abused his position of responsibility before God to commit adultery and murder. Just think about all those celebrity scandals that end up on the news: David's vices would light the blogosphere on fire today. But in ancient days, the next most public censure would have been Nathan's confrontation. If you were a beloved king accused by a well-respected prophet of heinous acts, you might have made your confession to God public, too. Going before God *and* a community of people whom you've wronged requires a sense of responsibility for your actions and a deep willingness to actively change.

Interestingly enough, the healing process can benefit from the same public exposure in the right circumstances. Take my experience, for example. Such an act of violence and the recovery afterward seems like it would be a story I keep to myself, a story I share with God and the people I love, and not the whole world willing to listen. But my story is anything but private. One little girl witnessed the attack, but a church witnessed the aftermath. The story was in the newspapers. You can Google me and still find articles. And my scars are far from hidden. Doctors evaluating my physical healing still ask, "What happened to you?" as if they hadn't just read the chart. Because God allowed me to be scarred so openly, so publicly, I've been testifying about what He's done to the world—and one by one exploring my own wounds and scars with people in conversation and my God on high. Because I have testified, God has healed me a little bit more every day.

Whether a confession or a testimony, glaringly public or forever hidden between you and God, your commitment to seeing yourself with painful clarity is the beginning of your transformation—a stage of forgiveness and healing that must always begin with an honest confession of who you are before God. In fact, there is some sense here that sins and scars now define who you are. It was there in front of David: when people looked at him, they saw the sin. And God wrote it in bold strokes all over me: when people look at me, they see my scars.

As the psalm progresses, David gets specific showing God his deep commitment; verse four moves to a deeper, more personal level of confession:

> *Against you, you only, have I sinned*
> *and done what is evil in your sight;*
> *so you are right in your verdict*
> *and justified when you judge.*

The sin of David is a social sin, committed against Bathsheba and against Uriah the Hittite, against the entire kingdom over which David ruled, against the community for which David was responsible. This is not a private sin. It is a very public one. And yet when he comes before God, he says that it is against God alone that he sinned.

Have you ever given God a thought when you commit a "social" sin? We offend and hurt people often enough in our lives that we're used to apologizing to them. Spreading hurtful gossip that happens to be true is a violation of social expectations, and you're likely to apologize to the friend you hurt with your loose tongue. But do you think to apologize to God? Sometimes we are more concerned with what people think of us and about saving face, than we are concerned with the fact that we have disappointed God more than our friend.

Of course, apologizing to other people is an expression of our repentance and our love and respect for them. But sin is theological, and this psalm says that ultimately all sin is sin against God. No matter whom you've hurt in the process, your relationship with God is really the heart of the problem. David knows Uriah is dead and that he'll need to find a way to make earthly amends, but he puts things into perspective first and seeks forgiveness from God before all else. This is all David's way of telling Nathan, "I know I have sinned and broken the law, but I first must go to my Father. He is the only one who knows; he's the only one who cares; he is the only one who can change this messed-up heart of mine. I know I've broken the law for man, but I answer to a higher power. I answer to the one who created me, the one who knows all about me, who knows my uprising and my downfall." David desired discipline.

Keeping things in decency and order when you seek healing is another matter entirely. Depending on the wound, earthly attention may be the only thing on your mind for a while. I certainly wasn't trying to define myself on the way to the hospital or in the early days of recovery. But there will always come a time when God is the port you need in your storm. What you can take away from this verse, though, is David-like determination to put God in charge of your healing.

He goes on to say:

> *Surely I was sinful at birth,*
> *sinful from the time my mother conceived me.*

Verse five is simply David's admission that he really is this bad; it could be the first time in his life he's ever been so honest. He is finally admitting, "I have never been much better than who I am at this moment."

You might be automatically nodding your head, but that admission is huge for this man. Put this confession against the background of David's life; perhaps it will give you perspective on how crucial this confession really is—for David, but also for us. As we read through the book of Samuel about the life of David, we are not prepared for what happens with Bathsheba. Everything that we have read about David up to that point says that this is truly a righteous person, that he truly is a man after God's own heart. Yet at that crucial moment, David committed the worst and most brutal kind of sin. He took his power as king, the power that was given to him by God to shepherd his people, and used it to abuse others. We just do not expect that in the David story. *David* didn't expect that in his story, either! Everyone is shocked that God's man is even *capable* of thinking such things, let alone actually doing them. "For as he thinks within himself, so he is" (Proverbs 23:7a).

If that proverb is tough for David, it's even tougher for us today. We as people of God do not like that kind of honesty about ourselves. We are very good at deceiving ourselves. We will do almost anything we have to do to avoid confronting who we really are. We *like* to think that we are righteous. We *like* to think that we're powerful enough to heal ourselves. But we're not—not if we're seeking total forgiveness and whole healing.

Here is where we need to start hearing the power of this psalm. Because after all, this psalm is not just about David. It is about us. The tragedy here is our tragedy as much as it is David's. This psalm is a challenge to that tendency we have of ignoring or refusing to see who we really are. It is a warning against seeing ourselves as so righteous before God, and so good that we are not willing to admit the immense potential that we have to sin.

Of course, our immediate reaction is, "Not me. I would never do that. " But that is the point here. We are just like David! This is a dangerous position to be in, because it overestimates who we are as human beings and underestimates the magnitude of the disruption, pain and sin that we can bring into the world just by our thoughts.

David was too good for this story; it shouldn't have happened to him. And yet one day, as he was simply out for a walk in the sunshine, the real David bubbled to the surface. And sooner or later, who we really are will come to the surface, as well. So look at yourself now and ask that question: "Who are you?" Don't shy from that answer nagging at the back of your mind—you know it's right.

Verse five tells us that, perhaps for the first time, the psalmist comes to the point of being able to see himself and is brought face to face with an ugly, cold image of himself. When we are confronted with who we really are, we are finally able to see what we are beyond all of our pretense to righteousness and strength. Beneath all the external veneer of goodness, where our will and intentions and motives hide, we really are that bad. Deep down, we're weak and bleeding out.

Don't be afraid of your feelings about what you're seeing: coming to this point is the only way that any newness can truly begin. As long as you believe that you're OK, there is no room for God to transform you. Only when you go honestly before God and yourself with the truth about who you really are can God begin working newness in your life. The first step toward light is to recognize the darkness.

The psalmist continues in verses six through nine and begins to unfold what needs to happen. A shift needs to happen, a complete 180, if you will:

> *Yet you desired faithfulness even in the womb;*
> *you taught me wisdom in that secret place.*
> *Cleanse me with hyssop, and I will be clean;*
> *wash me, and I will be whiter than snow.*
> *Let me hear joy and gladness;*
> *let the bones you have crushed rejoice.*
> *Hide your face from my sins*
> *and blot out all my iniquity.*

This section represents David's understanding of God's forgiveness. The symbols identified in the text are all the symbols of a priestly ritual of cleansing and renewal. For sinners, this passage is the promised magnitude of God's grace. For those with scars to bare, it's also a plea for rejuvenation and an acknowledgement of God's hand in *all things*.

Yet the psalm does not end here. If it did, David would seem content with asking for forgiveness for the sins he'd committed—even though he was a chosen leader. If the psalm ended here, we could concede that perhaps human sin is inevitable; only a cycle of penitent morning prayers after nights of debauchery would help us achieve God's favor. But verse ten takes us and David in a new direction for complete healing:

> *Create in me a pure heart, O God,*
> *and renew a steadfast spirit within me.*

You need to understand the radical change between verse nine and verse ten. Up to this point David has been talking about forgiveness, with all the liturgical and ritual language of washing and cleansing. This is the correct priestly language of what should happen when God forgives. Yet verse ten moves away from the language of the temple and the rituals, and so moves away from the language of forgiveness.

Notice there are different terms used here: "pure heart" and "steadfast spirit," to be exact. Something is different here. There is talk of newness, of new creation, not just the language of cleansing the old. And there is also the language of stability here, of a steadfastness that comes from within. This is the language of something more than forgiveness.

Part of the problem with forgiveness is that it can only deal with the results of sin. We must not minimize the nature of sin and the dimension of God's grace that makes forgiveness possible. Yet if we are not careful, it is easy to focus on the remedy for the sinful acts without ever asking what causes the sinful acts.

We can all too easily become trapped in a cycle of sin and forgiveness, so that we become more preoccupied with responding to sin than we are with being faithful to God in the first place. Sin is a matter of the heart and described in terms of unfaithfulness and disobedience. This suggests that a solution must involve the heart. How many times will God forgive? It is an easy question to ask, especially if we are talking about ourselves. We want to claim the fullness of God's grace easily, and affirm that his grace is unending. The more important question is, why should we keep sinning such that God has to forgive?

The language of creation in verse ten is particularly meaningful. In the Old Testament, the Hebrew word translated "create" is only used with God as the subject. Only God can bring the newness that the word "create" suggests. Here, there is no idea of washing the old heart and trying to remove the contamination of sin. The psalmist is no longer simply praying for continued forgiveness, but for a *radical* change in who he is.

If you are coming to this psalm with a spirit that

needs to be healed, this plea for re-creation may be exactly the type of help from God that you've been seeking. There comes a time when the pain and agony—whether physical or emotional—becomes too much to bear, and you're tired of being stitched up and bandaged back together. You may be strong in all things through Him, but He knows that when you come to Him with this prayer, something big has happened. Something that, whether you were ready for it or not, turned your world on end and opened you wide. This is the prayer of a woman who lost a child; of a man with nothing left to lose; of a child with no childhood left in sight. But it's not a prayer of defeat and desolation: you're asking the Lord to *renew* you. You're asking for a heart that doesn't burden you with pessimism. You're asking for a spirit that doesn't falter at the next test. You're crying, "Mold me, make me!"

In Hebrew, the "heart" is a metaphor for the seat of the intellect, the center of the will and decision-making. The "spirit" is also a metaphor for the entire person in terms of the motives and intentions that lie behind actions. To pray for a newly created heart and for a new spirit is a confession that the heart, the will of the person, is the source of the problem, the center of all pain and sin. Something has to happen beyond the forgiveness, something inside the heart that deals with who we are. So David cries out:

> *Do not cast me away from your presence*
> *or take your Holy Spirit from me.*

Here, as in all of the Old Testament, the "spirit" or "breath" of God is simply a way to talk about the presence of God in the world to effect change and growth. It is this "breath" of God that moved on the waters at the beginning of creation. It is this "breath" of God that dried up the waters of the Great Flood. It is this "breath" of God that filled Ezekiel's dry bones with new life. The prayer of the psalmist here is for the presence of God that will bring the change for which he cries. This is the only avenue to restoration and future stability, for which the psalmist prays in verse twelve:

Restore to me the joy of your salvation
and grant me a willing spirit, to sustain me.

The final transformation of the psalmist is on view in verse thirteen:

Then I will teach transgressors your ways,
so that sinners will turn back to you.

The psalmist is willing to share with others in teaching what he has himself learned about God. The one who was once nothing but a sinner, who had to face himself in light of where his sin had led him, can now envision turning with concern for other sinners. The one who stood at the brink of a failure of faith can be a well for the weary seeking His solace. The new heart for which the psalmist prays is not just to make him better. It is really a gift to the world. That newly created heart is a heart that beats for others, because it is a God-created heart.

Verse sixteen reveals more of what God wants in exchange for his forgiveness and healing:

You do not delight in sacrifice, or I would bring it;
you do not take pleasure in burnt offerings.

So we are to understand what God desires from us is not sacrifice and repentance, but transformation. David desires something greater than simply being forgiven of sin, and if we desire something more than forgiveness, then God desires something more for us as well. Verse sixteen shows that God grows as tired of our sacrifices and our repentance as we grow tired of offering them. What is the solution? Verse seventeen is a powerful conclusion in this psalm.

My sacrifice, O God, is a broken spirit;
a broken and contrite heart
you, God, will not despise.

What God wants is a person to come to a sense of brokenness in his or her life, just as the psalmist has done here. It is not just that we realize who we are, but that we are so grieved at who we are that we will cry out before God, "Make me new! I don't like who I am and I don't like what I have done. God, what I need is for you to do something new in my life that gives me a new heart, that so fills me with your presence that I can live a different way and be a different person."

That prayer can only come at the point of brokenness, when we come face to face with who we are, and do not like what we see. This is a brokenness that realizes that we cannot be the center of our world, even if we are king of Israel. It is a brokenness that knows if we are ever going to be different, we are going to have to give ourselves to God, to allow him to remake us on his terms. Talking of brokenness is hard, because it is scary to risk becoming something new, something unknown.

We have grown comfortable with ourselves, even though we know, in our better moments, that we are like the psalmist here. We would much rather have the joy of our religion. We would rather have all the blessings that go with being a Christian. I suspect that for many of us, we would much rather be trapped in the cycle of sin and forgiveness, hoping that who we really are is never exposed, than we would to become broken enough to have a new heart. Yet if we do not, we will never learn to love God with all of our heart, mind, soul and strength, nor will we ever learn to love our neighbor as ourselves. And these are the first two commandments from God!

As Christians, we often like to talk about Jesus dying on the cross for us, taking our place, but Jesus did not die on the cross so that you would not have to die. He died on that cross to show you the way to live—with purpose. You cannot get away from the idea of the cross! That cross is the kind of brokenness to which you are called when you take in your hands the symbols of His broken body and the cup of His suffering. If you are not willing to come before God with that kind of brokenness in yourself, a willingness to cry out to

God from a broken spirit for renewal, then you have not understood the Gospel. And you have not experienced the creative power that God can bring into your life.

Even through this doom and gloom of David's story and as you reflect on your story—even the parts you dare not share—God knows. And not only does He know: He cares. He desires for you to let go of your burdens, so you can get to verse fifteen. There is a place in this psalm for praise and rejoicing, and even for worship and sacrifice. Verse fifteen is about praise.

> *Open my lips, Lord,*
> *and my mouth will declare your praise.*

Praise your God even though you know you messed up, even though He alone knows and has seen that you've messed up. Praise your God even though you have suffered, even though you may not understand the purpose He has for you. Your sin and your pain might not be as public as David's, but they are there, hidden in your heart. They are blocking you from coming into true worship and fellowship and into complete praise with your God.

And don't look to others to judge the depth of your suffering or the depravity of your sin. You may not be like the woman in the Gospel who didn't stop bleeding for twelve years until she touched Jesus' robes. You may not be like that sister or that brother who admitted their addictions and their lustful spirits with the world and God before finding sobriety and forgiveness. But you've got something hidden in the crevasses of your heart, hidden away in your soul. You might protest that what you've been through isn't half of what they went through, but it's still keeping you from Him. And He knows your heart, the very essence of you. But if you cannot bring your burdens to Him, cannot look with honesty at your own self, can you answer that question nagging at your mind? "Who are you?"

Psalm 37:4 encourages you to "Take delight in the

Lord, and he will give you the desires of your heart." But before you can delight in God, you have to become broken in God. You decrease and let God increase, so that He will be glorified in your life. There can be no newness in Christian living that does not come out of brokenness. This is perhaps this psalm's most important insight into our own human existence. If you are not willing to come to that point of brokenness, there will be no new heart.

The only solution for your struggle is to come to the point where you are willing to face who you are honestly, to come to that crisis point in your life where you are willing to be recreated by God. That does not mean that everything will then be perfect. It does not mean there will be no more struggles in your life; after writing this psalm, David spent the rest of his life dealing with the unfolding consequences of his sin, and new heart or no, your scars will not leave you. But you *will* have a new heart that is steadfast and oriented to God. It means that you can have the very presence of God recreating you and transforming you by grace. It means you can have the living breath of God within you, giving you new life and enabling you to do what you cannot do on your own. That is the most important thing we learn about God from this psalm.

Do you believe that God can transform you? Do you believe that you can become "a child of God" living a life of holiness in perfect love toward God and others? As a believer, you need to remember Paul's words in Romans 8:35-37:

> *Who shall separate us from the love of Christ? Shall trouble or hardship or persecution or famine or nakedness or danger or sword? As it is written: 'For your sake we face death all day long; we are considered as sheep to be slaughtered.' No, in all these things we are more than conquerors through him who loved us.*

More than conquerors, meaning to have more than victory. To conquer something is to have the victory, but to be more than a conqueror we are to rejoice, for we have more than victory. There is *nothing* too hard for our God. And we respond to our struggles by crying out to God for newness from the midst of our brokenness. That cry is a cry of profound faith that is willing to place who we are in God's hands and let Him shape us however He wants. *Mold me and make me after thy will, while I am waiting, yielded and still.*

When we come to that point of crisis with the psalmist, and pray this prayer for a new heart from a broken spirit, we will never be the same. That's what a new heart means. This is whole healing, and the only one who can give us complete and whole healing is the one who created us from the beginning. It is a transformation by God of the very essence of who we are. He gives us a newly created heart first to love him, and then he will work in our lives to bring newness to us and others. This psalm is a call to new creation for your soul.

The Challenge. On July 22, 2007, I thought I was whole, I thought I had it going on; but God had to do something drastic to get my heart. He had to do spiritual surgery. While the plastic surgeon performed the surgery on my body, God was creating in me a new heart. I was a victim and a survivor for a moment. But I am forever more than a conqueror.

Live beyond what has happened to you. You are not to be defined by your shortcomings and trials. Look at that moment that hurt you, and realize it was only for a moment. You cannot allow a mere moment to define who you are and to keep you from praising your God, no matter how public or how personal it may be. I challenge you to move beyond yourself, beyond who you are right now. I challenge you to have a one-on-one conversation with God. Your whole healing is personal to God, so put yourself in God's way and let Him intentionally break you into little pieces.

Exodus 4:12

"Now go; I will help you speak and will teach you
what to say."

PART III
VOICES IN UNISON

9 | Defending the Sanctuary

by Reverend F. Dorsey Houston

PSALM 5:11

"But let all who take refuge in you be glad; let them ever sing for joy. Spread your protection over them that those who love your name may rejoice in you."

Churches should always be free to ring with joyous singing and raucous praise to God; in quiet moments, churches should soothe the troubled and lift up in prayer those in need. But too often this chaotic world around us rises up, and darker forces lay siege to the houses of the faithful. Once refuges for anyone seeking His comfort, churches are now targets of violence, depravity and heartache.

As a former legal investigator, corporate security officer, church security director and chief armor bearer, I've seen a lot of situations where—if security and safety procedures were in place—many terrible situations could have been prevented. This subject of church security is nothing new, though: in biblical times soldiers were assigned to guard the gates, palaces and synagogues. The difference today is that many ministries are too laidback when it comes to having a safe, secure worship experience. Anointed to Protect and Serve Ministries, Inc., was born over five years ago to educate modern churches in the simple procedures they can put in place to protect their congregation and property. We offer the "Sanctuary Defense" Church Security Seminar and Workshop to churches nationwide, in hopes that our expertise can save lives and keep churches of all sizes safe for their communities.

Our comprehensive, on-site, two-day workshop begins with an orientation to church safety and security and the basics a church would need to start a program at their worship center. As many church officers and members have little security experience, it's important that basic details like the dynamics of a security detail and leadership skills are covered early on.

Day One also addresses several specific emergency concerns, including sanctuary fire safety and cyber defense. We also conduct a Security Threat Assessment that inspects areas such as the parking lot, hourly patrols before, during and after services, vehicle monitoring, abandoned vehicles and what an exterior security detail should look for on patrol. This way, a church security team of any level of experience gets an expert assessment of the systems in place and the facilities available to allow for more improvement. We also spend some time working through specific safety and security scenarios to get the security team used to working together on the church grounds.

Hands-on training continues in the second day, including one-on-one assessments with team members, and setting patrol positions in and outside the sanctuary. It's important to recognize that a safety or security issue could arise from anywhere on or off the church grounds. Teams need to know how to prepare for and react to any type of situation. We also ensure that team members understand several highly important issues that balance legal and security matters, including:

1) the rights of Church officials (including security) to physically remove a disruptive person from the church premises.

2) the duty of the Church to protect worshipers, including effecting of personal protection or restraining orders entered against a person on church property.

3) the constitutional right to enter a church for the purpose of worship, though this right is far from absolute.

4) the Church's right to bar and/or physically remove a person from its property and services if the person is engaging in disruptive conduct.

Where any security training might teach you these basics, we make sure to integrate church concerns, including making the security efforts a fully integrated ministry and developing a servant's spirit. We also stress the importance of a volunteer screening program (including a background check) and reasonable standards to be imposed on volunteer security personnel. While any member can volunteer to serve, every church should consider the safety of its congregation and its legal liability when accepting a volunteer. Churches should also have a public relations program with an administrator trained to handle press relations in an emergency situation.

But most importantly, before we can talk about protecting the church, we need protection first. We must have a relationship with our God, and have the peace of mind salvation brings before facing life's challenges.

With our God and our members protecting our churches, our sanctuaries will be safer havens than ever.

TEN CHURCH SAFETY AND SECURITY ISSUES
YOU'LL WANT TO TALK TO YOUR PASTOR ABOUT

1. Child Safety Protocol
2. Volunteer Screening Protocol
3. Fire Evacuation Plan
4. Severe Weather Evacuation Plan
5. Security Threat Evacuation Plan
6. Cyber Threat Safety Protocol
7. Identity Theft Prevention Protocol
8. Event Safety/Security Plan
9. Food Safety Protocol
10. Visitor Protocol

10 | DEFENDING THE MIND

by Laverne Williams

HOSEA 4:6

"My people are destroyed from lack of knowledge."

Yolanda Cooper's story is not unique. In fact, it is all too common. Some of us may not look like Ms. Cooper or would never commit such a drastic offense, but many of us are dealing with some form of emotional challenge and may be not so far away from losing control as she did.

Seeking help from a psychiatrist or psychologist is usually not an option we in communities of faith will consider. Surveys I have personally conducted and other studies show that many African American women rely on supports other than mental health services. There is a strong reliance on community, the support of family and the religious community during periods of emotional distress. Black women seek mental health care less than white women and, when we do seek it, do so later in life and at more severe stages of disease. Some delay treatment so long that admission to a psychiatric hospital is inevitable, whereas early detection could have offered outpatient treatment as an option. Adding to the dilemma is the fact that only 2% of psychiatrics, 2% of psychologists and 4% of clinical social workers in the United States are African American. That's not many to go around!

An important fact is that the small percentage of persons seeking professional health services has caused mental health professionals to *under*-diagnose disorders like depression and *over*-diagnose disorders like schizophrenia in the African American community. This is due, in part, to the fact that African Americans metabolize medications at a different rate compared to whites, yet do not remain in treatment long enough to receive the right dosage.

Other facts:

Statistics show that more than 2.5 million African Americans have bipolar disease.

Only 7% of African American women with depression seek help.

Twice as many women as men experience depression.

Consider this scenario: The person in church sitting right next to or near you on Sunday morning is crying and you think, "Wow, God is touching her/his heart" or "that song the choir or soloist is singing must be one of their favorites." Go one step further: What about Sister Canada, who wears a new suit, hat and shoes just about every week, has a wonderful loving husband, lives in a beautiful home with a white picket fence, has 2.5 children, and drives a Lexus? She looks like she's got it all together, right? Surely our Lord has smiled upon her and her family. Hmmmm.

Don't let the outside appearance deceive you. She may be what I refer to as one of the "Walking Wounded" — going through the motions, but underneath there is something not quite right about how she feels that she can't put a name to.

As African American females, we also have a large tendency to talk to "our girl" when we have challenges. Now don't get me wrong, I am all for having someone to bounce my feelings off of, but you need to recognize when your "girl" needs help herself! After all, how many times have you heard, "None of our family members had to go to a psychiatrist or psychologist. They just prayed, read their bibles and endured it"? Or "We got through slavery, we can get through anything"? Beware! If you look closely at her situation, you may find a woman who is perhaps not sleeping at night, missing work on a consistent basis, isolating herself from her friends, complaining of constant headaches or going to her medical doctor to treat aches and pains that cannot be physically explained.

The shame of admitting you may have a mental illness exacerbates barriers of seeking help like:

- Denial

- Embarrassment

- Don't want/refuse help

- Lack money/insurance

- Fear

- Lack knowledge of treatment/problem

- Hopelessness

Not long after this horrific incident, Pastor Jonathan Whitfield learned of the PEWS (Promoting Emotional Wellness & Spirituality) program at the Mental Health Association in New Jersey, of which I am the director, and urged his congregation to attend a session. They readily agreed and rapidly gained knowledge of emotional wellness.

As a social worker and a deacon, and having had challenges myself with anxiety, I now find my life's mission is to raise awareness in communities of color about the synergistic relationship between emotional and spiritual wellness and breaking down the barriers that prevent us from seeking mental health treatment. Even as a social worker, I found it difficult to reach out for help. Growing up in the 1950s had not prepared me to go to anyone other than my pastor or the deacon in charge of my family. When scheduling appointments with clergy, most congregants are not aware that psychology is not a large part of the seminary curriculum, which could make clergy uncomfortable discussing psychological issues.

With this in mind and as an African American woman, I founded Laverne Williams Enterprise, LLC, a consulting firm that provides individually tailored emotional health, wellness and spiritual workshops for various faith communities and organizations. I explore many topics with my clients including an overview of emotional wellness, signs and symptoms of mental health issues, crisis intervention, wellness and recovery, and treatment options.

The MHANJ investigated how to partner with faith-based institutions as an avenue to expand access to mental health services for the African American community. In meeting with members of a number of churches, it was very clear that little or no mental health training existed for the ministry and lay people, although it is the lay people who provide a clear majority of outreach within congregations.

The structure of the church usually does not provide the direction, education and support that those with mental health concerns need in order to effectively address their issues. Most church leaders we interviewed believed that the church needed to be more active in helping people access the mental health system and educating people about the emotional needs of the community.

The PEWS Program began in 2005 with the purpose of publicizing a positive message of mental health and wellness to persons of color and to faith communities. Our goals included educating clergy in ways to effectively support congregants who have, or may be at risk of developing, a mental illness, to fight the stigma often associated with mental illness within these communities and to more aggressively open the doors of mental health treatment providers for individuals struggling with emotional challenges. The PEWS Ministry consists of:

> **Award-winning videos** that tell the moving stories of individuals with emotional challenges, the role spirituality plays in their lives, and their experiences with their families and their religious communities.

PowerPoint presentations and interactive discussions that focus on the relationship between spiritual wellness and emotional wellness.

Training and Technical Assistance for PEWS Mental Health Ministries that introduces church clergy, lay leaders, heads of ministries and congregants to ways they can help those who may be struggling with emotional wellness issues, and assists them with identifying appropriate community resources and services to which they can link people.

A PEWS Ministry can be a "stand-alone" ministry that is focused specifically on congregants with mental health issues, or it can be incorporated into an already existing health ministry. This decision rests solely on the leadership of the church.

There is no health without good mental health.

Given the fact that the world's major religions view helping those who are suffering as a core value of their institutions, and that people who are suffering often seek out their spiritual mentors in times of crisis, bringing education and training about emotional wellness and its connection to overall wellness to faith-based communities is a much-needed service. The church is where many African Americans seek spiritual, physical and emotional health. Church members becoming better educated about persons who have a mental illness, and how to help or show them how to help themselves, are enacting the commission of Jesus (and other major world religious leaders)—to support, love and care for one another.

Steps your congregation can take to become more aware and sensitive to persons who are experiencing emotional challenges are:

- Contact community mental health service providers and enlist their help in educating your congregation.

- Establish relationships with chaplains in prisons and psychiatric hospitals to build bridges to faith communities as part of discharge planning.

- Advocate from the pulpit and the pews that spiritual practices should be regarded as a complement, rather than a *substitute*, for proper medical care.

- Train church security to identify someone who is experiencing a mental health crisis.

- Invite spiritual leaders to join in the development and implementation of community mental health initiatives.

- Train Sunday school teachers how to identify "at-risk youth" and how to provide families with resources.

- Have pastors recommend theological seminaries that include psychological first aid as part of their training.

Laverne Williams Enterprise, LLC, can assist you with this knowledge by revealing how emotional and spiritual wellness do not have to compete with one another but can work together to help each individual reach the highest degree of spiritual, emotional and physical wellness.

Members of churches are often trying to cope with one or more life-altering challenges at a time—from issues such as addiction, depression, domestic violence, trauma and involvement with the criminal justice system to providing dignified care to elders, giving consistent supervision to at-risk youth and dealing with issues of grief and loss. Sadly, many of these struggles that our communities face are pervasive and affect almost all churches on some level.

Raising awareness, creating PEWS Mental Health Ministries, hosting conferences on the connection between emotional wellness and spirituality, and training pastors and lay leaders about mental health issues are good places to start.

What happened to Lady Whitfield cannot be undone. But we can make it our business to recognize the warning signs so that others do not experience the same terrifying experience. Let's make Theresa's remarkable resiliency count for something!

CONCLUSION

LIVING BOLDLY FOR CHRIST

Something inside me knows that if I didn't have my scars, I wouldn't remember the attack as vividly as I do. Every now and then, my upper lip goes numb, and I have to feel for it before I remember there's a scar there. Other days, I itch my scars contentedly, enjoying the little burning reminder that I've been *remade* by a merciful God who has a purpose for me.

Not long after I'd begun this book, my husband and our children took me out to dinner for Mother's Day. When we were all settled at the table with our meals, he asked each one to share why they love me. For a moment, I was worried. My children had seen so many things in *my* life over the years, had struggled with their own questions and worries after the attack. I was admittedly *scared* of what they would say... But I'll never forget their answers.

"Mommy is a loving and beautiful person."

"She can come off strong sometimes, but she means well. What she says usually works out. It helps us, and we look back and realize that the words she gave us were good words."

Then Christopher, my oldest, said, "My mom made me who I am today. She gives me good strong words. I'm a strong man because of my mother."

I started to cry. Had I really been able to raise this incredible young man? Had I really found a way to fight through the turmoil and find solid ground for myself and my children? A door closed behind me; I was through the wilderness.

Every time I tell my story, I know I'm talking to women who have walked the same tortured trails that I have. I know I'm sharing His message with people who are broken and searching for a way to heal, for the same freedom I've found. If I can inspire or encourage someone along my journey, my living—and my nearly dying—shall not be in vain. To God be the glory!

AFTERWORD
Arm Yourself for the Lord
by Pastor Jonathan Whitfield

PSALM 39:2-5

So I remained utterly silent,
not even saying anything good.
But my anguish increased;
my heart grew hot within me.
While I meditated, the fire burned;
then I spoke with my tongue:

"Show me, LORD, my life's end
and the number of my days;
let me know how fleeting my life is.
You have made my days a mere handbreadth;
the span of my years is as nothing before you.
Everyone is but a breath,
even those who seem secure."

It's been a trying time.

Two or three years before the attack, Trinity started showing up on Satan's radar. We were moving and shaking and breaking out into the community to do good. But we had no Peters keeping watch over the sanctuary, no armor bearers looking out for myself or my wife or anyone in the congregation. If only we had opened our eyes, we might have seen something bigger coming.

My campaign to move my church from membership to discipleship started with service. Christ has said the work of the church is to serve those who are less fortunate than we are. It doesn't matter if you're starting a prison ministry or a hospice ministry or something in-between: He says that if they lack the resources, the church is to give aid. And we serve our seniors—the people who raised us—and the children, who will one day take care of us in return. And of course, this leads us into helping sinners get saved. In every way, we're acting as our brothers' keepers. When we're doing these things, I know we're doing God's work. I can't promise the choir member that when they're singing, they're doing God's work. I can't promise that every preacher is even in the right mindset to do His will on the pulpit. There may not be a set of verses that says it plainer than Matthew 7:21-23:

> *"Not everyone who says to me, 'Lord, Lord,' will enter the kingdom of heaven, but only the one who does the will of my Father who is in heaven. Many will say to me on that day, 'Lord, Lord, did we not prophesy in your name and in your name drive out demons and in your name perform many miracles?' Then I will tell them plainly, 'I never knew you. Away from me, you evildoers!'"*

It's plain to see that the things we do for our churches are nothing, in God's eyes, when compared to what He wants us to do for humanity.

It only makes sense, then, that the attack came as we were on the cusp of making a difference for God. Satan reached out and attacked my heart, attacked my family; he did exactly what he knew would threaten to cripple my resolve in the Lord.

The weekend of the attack, I'd traveled to Maryland to visit a friend of mine and to preach for him, but I took two brothers with me so that we could observe, evaluate and interview his security ministry. With all the work we'd been doing out in the world, we were opening our doors to a whole host of people with problems we didn't always understand, but wanted to help anyway. Worst of all, we couldn't always recognize the extent of a problem, never knowing if belligerence was a symptom to worry about or to dismiss as simply disrespectful. Knowing my friend's ministry could help ours, I was excited to bring back information on a security ministry for Trinity and to formally create positions for armor bearers and other protectors within the church.

So when I got the call telling me that Theresa had been attacked, I almost felt as if I'd had a premonition of something going wrong. I felt like I'd been caught unawares, like I hadn't moved quick enough to skirt Satan's sword. Even worse, I questioned whether I was able to truly protect my family. I felt undeserving and reduced and beaten. What kind of man can't protect and provide for his family? I wondered on that long drive back to New Jersey.

When I got to the hospital, I set my questions for myself aside. I immediately tried to pour all of my energy into securing Theresa's recovery. I wanted to make sure that she was okay, that the surgery had gone well. I wanted to make sure that she knew she was going to be all right. I wanted to make sure she had everything she needed. I was trying to be the best husband I could be in this situation, and her best friend, too. I wanted to accentuate everything we'd meant to each other, so that our relationship would be one sure thing in her life. But to be that man, I needed to let the macho go. I let my own hurt go; I let the inconsistency go. Everything negative I'd been feeling about myself and my role as a husband, I put that aside for a while. I wanted to pour myself into Theresa, and I did that.

About week three, when the physical recovery was really starting to take place and we could start to see Theresa getting better, I allowed myself to look inside to my own questions and fears. It had been weeks since I'd tried to face the emotional repercussions, tried to put back together the pieces that were in me. I had to try to think rationally who I was as a man and what this attack said about me as a husband. I had barely started piecing things together when the nightmares started. I felt totally violated by the attack. My trust in the power of our work as a church was shaken. My confidence that my family was safe was shattered. My assurance, even, that my church was safe faltered. I dreamed about doing the most horrible things. Beyond being hurt, I was angry. I wanted to hurt the woman who hurt my wife. And the images were so brutal and real, and my anger was so overpowering, I started to wonder whether or not I could return to the church for fear that I, too, would lose control one day.

And with that first question came a flood of others: "God why? I'm doing what you said! I'm actually doing it by the book; I'm actually trying to help the hurt! Lord, if you're supposed to protect me and I'm shouting this from the pulpit, how do I deal with this as a person? I get tears in my eyes just looking at my wife, and my kids are crying, and yet I'm trying to be strong. How can I be the man and keep my family together? And even when my family is healed, my church is looking for me to come back because I'm the pastor—but how do I come back and promote you when personally right now I feel like you let me down? How am I going to go back on the screen for you, when I know I was doing your job and I know I was serving the people you say should be served, and now look what happened?"

I had great difficulty returning to the discipleship campaign, even though I knew it was right. Had I been the one attacked, I could have easily given it straight to Jesus for the cause. I knew that as a soldier for Him, I would be putting myself in a vulnerable position, as any soldier should. But I was not the one in that bathroom that day: my wife and child were. The thought of losing them… it made me ask some important questions about my purpose and the consequences it could have on the lives of the people I love. At that point, it wasn't about being a pastor: it was about being Jonathan—about being the man He needs me to be.

I didn't know what to do with all my hurt except take it back to Him. I found great comfort in the Word—specifically Job and Psalm 39. Like me, Job questioned everything and found that he had no one to question except God Himself. Theresa and I both found healing power in that particular book and were reminded of the part one person's suffering can play in the bigger picture of God's plan. And in Psalm 39, David just shouts to God in anguish and confusion. God doesn't answer David in that psalm like He often does: David just screams and vents, and when it's all over, his faith kicks back in.

Just like He was the only one I could scream to, He was also the only one I could turn to for answers. I knew He would be the one to reenergize me, if anyone could. I knew that He would be the one to refill my bag of tricks, so to speak. I knew if my mind would be full of good things to say concerning Him, He'd be the one to do it. I knew that if God were real, He'd need to do for me exactly what He did for Job if ever I'd be qualified and blessed for ministry. Only God could be the source of my recovery and the decision-maker sending me back to this battlefield.

And that's what He did, through the course of time. I read His word; I prayed and talked to Him. I didn't confide in many people about my healing, and only sought two fellow ministers who saw I was deeply with God and were willing to merely hold me to Him rather than counsel and direct me with their opinions. They kept sending me back to Him and let me work out my own troubles. And all the while, Theresa was the catalyst for my healing.

Her attitude from the day after the attack forward helped Pastor Whitfield stay in the faith and gave Jonathan the means of looking at this thing from a spiritual perspective, not just a literal one. She helped me get over my hurt pride and my self-destructive attitude. Theresa helped me catch a glimpse of how fragile and volatile *all* life can be — not just the life of a battling pastor. She's a woman with a remarkable attitude who led me through my darkness by example. She made me seek God harder than I ever have before. My wife will forever be my hero.

✦　✦　✦　　　　✦　✦　✦

Some mornings I wake up still surprised to find that it wasn't all a dream. The numbness and shock still come; I don't think you ever get over it. We live our lives constantly on guard, when our neighbors are calm, confident and comfortable. I've had military training and I've always felt able to defend myself and my family, but Yolanda Cooper's attack on my wife—in my own church—made me start looking at briefcases and bulging coats with suspicion. Now I pay attention to weather conditions and clothing, strange and unusual movements, appearances, conversations, looks... Anything that could indicate a threat to my family or my parishioners puts me on edge.

I am not the only one watching, either. Our church leaders have their eyes open. They've been charged with spreading awareness and developing the resources to keep our church safe. The parishioners share our sense of urgency, because it's no longer something that happened on the other side of the country—it happened in our backyard, to someone we know, someone we love!

From our awareness, a security ministry was born. Through it, the atmosphere in our church has changed. There is no longer a blind freedom to just come in and do anything without being checked first. Any visitor can clearly see that there is a presence working to maintain order. I have armor bearers, now—as does my wife—and our church's perimeter is patrolled. The men who serve us remind me of Peter. He was the disciple ready and willing to literally fight and protect the cause, never more so than in the Garden of Gethsemane. Jesus may have told him to set aside his sword then, but there had been times before when Peter's role as guardian had been essential to preserving the life and ministry of Christ and the apostles. Jesus must have known who his protector was, and churches need to take the time to identify their Peters too. These ready and willing men need to be empowered righteously to guard and protect the sanctuaries, the conferences, the choir rooms, the women's meetings, the usher's meetings, the children's classes. Any time the church's doors are open, there should be a host of Peters keeping safety in mind.

But these good citizens stand great tests in their service — tests church leaders need to expect and prepare to overcome. What of those serving with the security ministries who don't have military or police training? How many of those members will feel prepared and confident enough to disarm an armed stranger rushing for the pulpit? I know I was taught to meet aggression with aggression, but most members wouldn't be prepared to defend the church in those types of situations without risking their lives. When a church is able, members of security ministries need to be trained as thoroughly as possible — from hand-to-hand to hand-to-arm combat and back again. And whenever possible, a church should utilize members who have been professionally trained for such measures. Whether veterans or police officers, these volunteers will take up the banner even in the situations you can't anticipate. I would even be comfortable with an undercover officer armed on church grounds, solely for the purpose of being able to confidently stride up to a belligerent person and intervene.

And what of the ushers, you might ask? They have always been the people maintaining order in the sanctuary, and they should still be present. When I was a kid, the ushers were constantly checking everything: if someone was chewing gum or passing notes or standing up to go to the bathroom, the ushers were there. They'd rap kids' knuckles, run notes across the sanctuary discreetly, even offer help to any adult who seemed out of touch with the service. Now, they should support security by keeping the parishioners in order. A security officer doesn't need to worry about children kicking seatbacks or cell phones ringing; in the same way, an usher shouldn't need to worry about looking for suspicious characters. But in a crisis, they should both be prepared to work together.

Even greater than the challenges a church will face in the event of a violent attack, the church needs to realize exactly what it's up against in serving humanity. The Bible clearly states that Satan is our opposition. He constantly wants to devastate us: he is for our destruction and not our construction. Knowing the enemy is so powerful and so cunning, we must widen our perspective. Satan is not just silently sitting by while we arm our willing parishioners; he is among us, influencing us. Our first instinct is not to see Satan's hand in it, though. No, first we see the face of the person discouraging us or working against us. Ephesians 6:12 reminds us that our battles will more often be subtle than they will be obvious: "For our struggle is not against flesh and blood, but against the rulers, against the authorities, against the powers of this dark world and against the spiritual forces of evil in the heavenly realms." I think if we can really begin to realize what the Scripture has been trying to tell us about Satan and his spiritual warfare, we'll be awakened.

God has even told us how prepared we need to be as His soldiers. 1 Peter 5:8 says, "Be alert and of sober mind. Your enemy the devil prowls around like a roaring lion looking for someone to devour." It means that we're not supposed to be sleepwalking. We're supposed to realize that the closer we get to the coming of Jesus, the more intense this battle is going to get between good and evil. Knowing that the battle would get worse, Jesus even reminded us that he was preparing us long ahead of time: "And on this rock I will build my church, and the gates of Hades will not overcome it" (Matthew 16:18). And most people hear Jesus' words and expect that the gates of hell will be coming for the church at any moment. What they forget is that the church is on the move. We're *working* to reconcile God and his people, and our work draws notice—so Satan must work against us to keep us from moving. Evil isn't among us until we've got something right. When Satan knows a church is a threat, that's when he moves in.

Now, I said all that just to say this: the biggest issues the church faces today, from the lack of fear or reverence for God to the lack of fear or reverence for God's leaders, are all part of this warfare. Even freedom is a problem when people are free to come into our church at will and attack the men, women and children of God. All of these things are in this background of every service and class. These evil influences are the things that we're fighting against, not specific people with specific faces. If only we'd wake up and see that these challenges aren't just the making of the modern world, of changing times. Only when we're ready to battle for the Lord will we serve His purpose and plan. In my church, I call it moving from membership to discipleship. Satan probably thinks of it as painting a target on our backs.

Many churches never think about security because they're never on the battlefield. A soldier doesn't need a gun if he isn't going to fight, so if a church is going to just live comfortably and operate more like a club, what security do they really need? If they're focused on ushers days and nurses days and choir days, and that's all they're going to do, what risk is there? If they never open up their doors to the mentally ill and say, "Come unto me all ye that labor and are heavy laden and I will give you rest," they'll never need to think about the baggage their visitors may be dragging in. Really, from whom would they even be protecting themselves—each other? Churches who only do work for the church hardly even give the devil an opportunity to work his evil; they're no threat to him! With active, fighting churches to worry about, it's almost like Satan says, "I don't need to bother you because you're not *doing* anything."

The churches that *need* and *have* security aren't overstating their own importance. I don't have twelve men around me because I'm a rock star. They're with me because

I lead the church onto the battlefield. We do have an enemy, and that enemy desires, as the Scriptures say, to kill, steal and destroy. If we do this work and stick our necks out, we make ourselves vulnerable by serving our community. One book out right now reminds us that "Hurt people hurt people"; we *know* that we are taking risks, so we need to protect the gifted and purpose-driven people in our communities.

That protection of God's purpose is truly the heart of a security ministry. It doesn't matter how popular or influential a pastor or First Lady is: it's about the work any gifted person in a church is doing. If we are really out there to make a difference in a lasting way, we need to make sure the people He intended to serve Him do not die before their time at the hands of the devil. Jesus didn't die until it was time, though there had been many opportunities for Satan to do his worst. At the Last Supper, he even told his disciples times were going to get tough and commanded them to arm themselves in preparation. Jesus made good use of his courageous servant Peter, and didn't stop Peter from protecting him until the very end when it was Jesus' time to go.

✦   ✦   ✦   ✦   ✦   ✦

Though I have healed, I am far from the man I was before. When I see a church resisting the simplest precautions for their safety, it *hurts*. The fact that so many people have been touched by stories like ours — or worse — and yet churches still deny the need for security takes away from the impact of the sacrifices of those caught unawares before them. As time goes by, as stories across the country replace the ones in our own backyard, a sense of urgency in the community dwindles, and I find myself frustrated at how quickly some people can forget.

I don't think my urgency and my sense of vulnerability will ever go away, and I don't think it should. I've learned to balance it with a degree of trust, faith and hope for our journey. To live in constant worry or fear is not the life I'd wish for myself or my church. Trinity's future is in the world outside our doors still, whether Satan is targeting us or not. If he does, I pray we continue to do all that we can to protect ourselves against him, and I leave the rest in God's most capable hands.

I know that God is blessing my future, piece by piece. Before the attack and my own tumultuous healing process, I believed that my pastoring fueled my person—that Pastor Whitfield just happened to be Jonathan as well. Now, I think my person is fueling my pastoring. The "Jonathan" part of me has a real sense—without a title, without a job—that God is real, that God loves me, that God wants to use me. In that very real sense, my salvation relationship is now fueling my ministry. I'm not doing things because I'm a pastor; I'm doing it because I'm a *disciple*. I'm an individual who knows the Lord. He's put this responsibility of pastoring on me, but He's given the strength of faith—and His armor to bear—to this guy called Jonathan. And I am proud to celebrate these scars.

Recommended Reading

In my time of soul-searching and healing, I have turned to the Lord so many times, and He has in turn sent me some great words of wisdom and testimonies of faith. Sometimes the trials of others can help us see our own path more clearly. I pray these books that have so blessed me in my times of need will find room in your heart and mind, helping you to celebrate who you are and the great God who has made you that way!

The Holy Bible

Breaking the Silence

Author: Dr. Kim Yancey James

ISBN: 978-1450048552

Remember to Breathe

Author: Dawn Breedon

ISBN: 978-0977110612

Why Forgive?

Author: Johann Christoph Arnold

ISBN: 978-0874869064

Brokenness: The Forgotten Factor of Prayer

Author: Mickey Bonner

ISBN: 978-1878578129

The Five Star Church:

Author: Stan Toler, Alan E. Nelson

ISBN: 978-0830723508

CONTACT LADY THERESA WHITFIELD

To contact Lady Whitfield, you may email her directly at:

Jtckfamily@aolcom

Or you may reach her through Trinity Baptist Church:

218 Passaic Street

Hackensack, NJ

Telephone: (201) 487-3656

Website: trinitybch.org

R&B Group Days

Married!

Date Night

Expecting

Portrait of Love

The New Addition

THE ATTACK

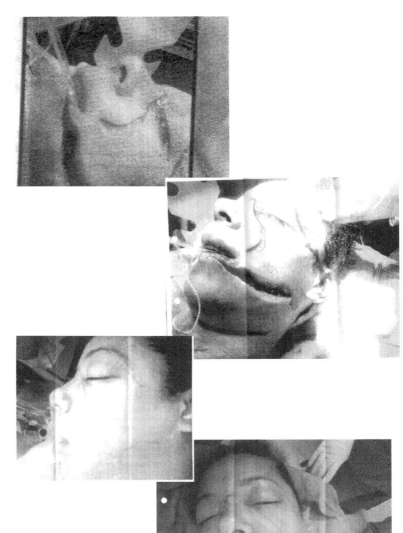

CELEBRATING MY SCARS

18769594R00077

Made in the USA
Charleston, SC
20 April 2013